Workbook

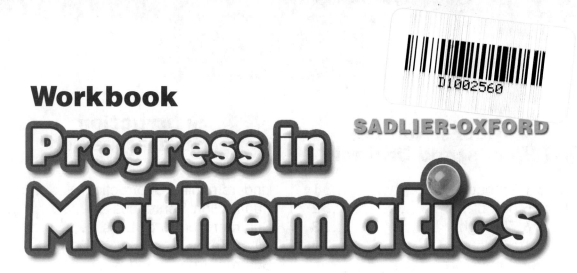

Progress in Mathematics

SADLIER-OXFORD

Catherine D. LeTourneau

with

Elinor R. Ford

Sadlier-Oxford
A Division of William H. Sadlier, Inc.
www.sadlier-oxford.com

Contents

iii

Measurement

Add 2-Digit Numbers

Subtract 2-Digit Numbers

Fractions and Probability

Numbers 1 Through 4

Numbers show how many.

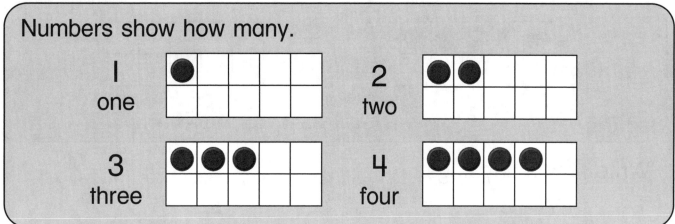

How many bugs?
Write the number word and the number.

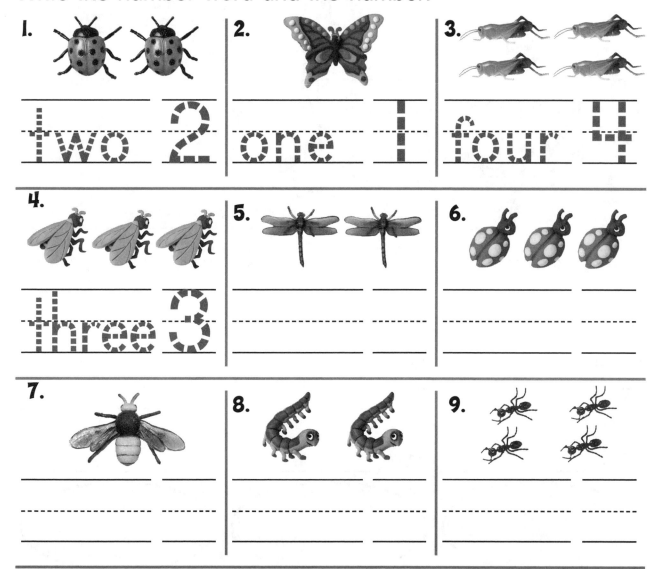

Numbers 5 and 0

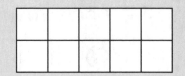 5 five   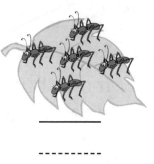 0 zero

Write how many bugs.

1.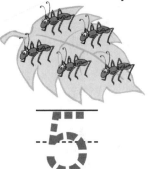
5

2.
0

3.
_____
- - - - - - - -
_____

Write the number word and the number.

4.
five 5

5.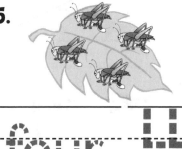
four 4

6.
_____
- - - - - - - -
_____

Write the number word.
Draw dots for each number.

7. 5 _____

8. 0 _____

9. 4 _____

Numbers
6 Through 9

Name _____

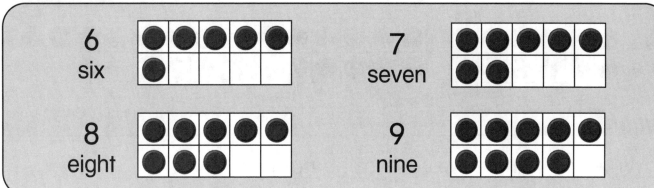

6 six
7 seven
8 eight
9 nine

Write the number word and the number.

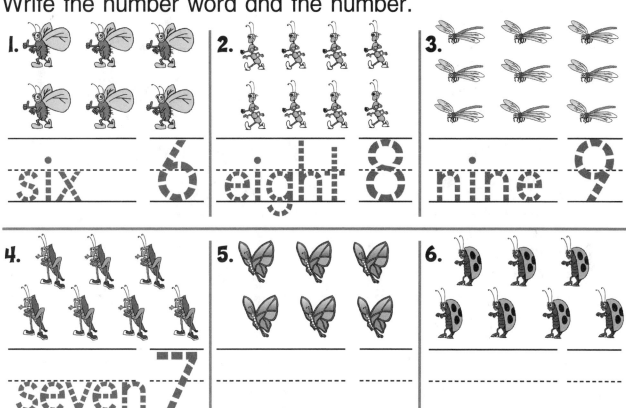

1. six 6

2. eight 8

3. nine 9

4. seven 7

5. _____ _____

6. _____ _____

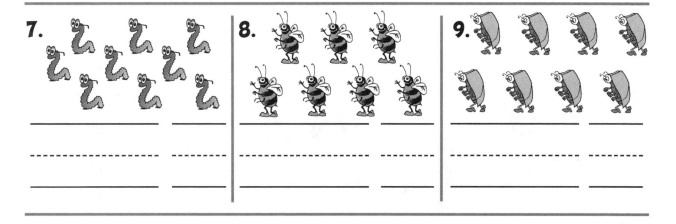

7. _____ _____

8. _____ _____

9. _____ _____

Numbers
10 Through 12

Name _____

 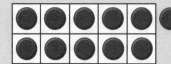 10 ten

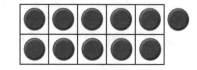  11 eleven   12 twelve

Write the number word and the number.

1.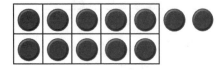

twelve 12

2.

eleven 11

3.

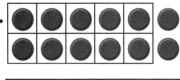
ten 10

4.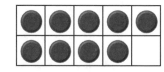

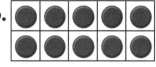 
nine 9

Write the number word.

5.

_____

- - - - - - - - - - - -

_____

6.

_____

- - - - - - - - - - - -

_____

7.

_____

- - - - - - - - - - - -

_____

8. **10**

_____

- - - - - - - - - - - -

9. **11**

_____

- - - - - - - - - - - -

10. **12**

_____

- - - - - - - - - - - -

Use with Lesson 4, text pages 9–10.

One Fewer, One More Name _____

3 ☐ is one fewer than 4 ■. | 5 ☐ is one more than 4 ■.

Draw one more. Write the number.

1.

2.

_____
- - - - - - - -
_____

3.

_____
- - - - - - - -
_____

4.

_____
- - - - - - - -
_____

✗ to show one fewer. Write the number.

5.

6.

_____
- - - - - - - -
_____

7.

_____
- - - - - - - -
_____

8.

_____
- - - - - - - -
_____

Order
0 Through 12

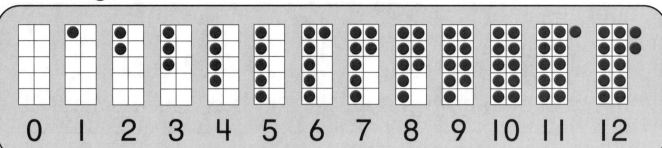

0   1   2   3   4   5   6   7   8   9   10   11   12

Write how many. Then order the numbers.

1. 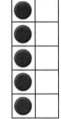 5   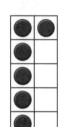 ___   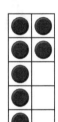 ___   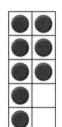 ___

____, ____, ____, ____

2.  ___    ___   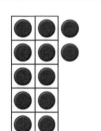 ___   ___

____, ____, ____, ____

Write the missing numbers.

3. 4, 5, 6, ____

4. ____, 9, 10, ____

5. ____, 3, ____, 5

6. ____, ____, 2, 3

7. ____, 10, 11, ____

8. 6, ____, ____, 9

Count On

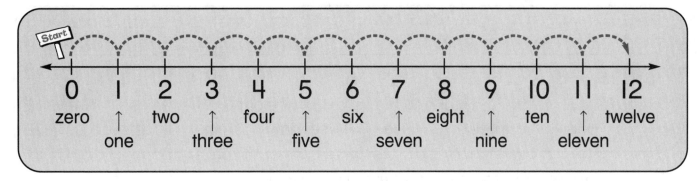

Count on. Write the missing numbers.

1.

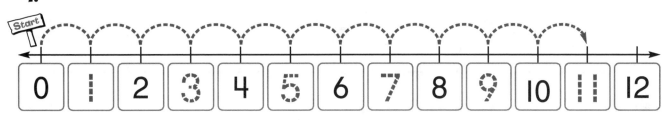

2.

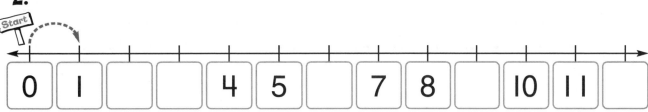

3.

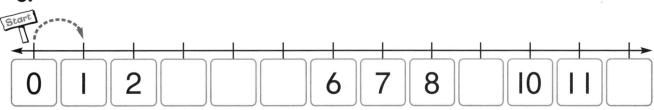

4.

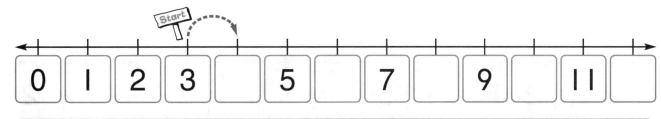

Count Back

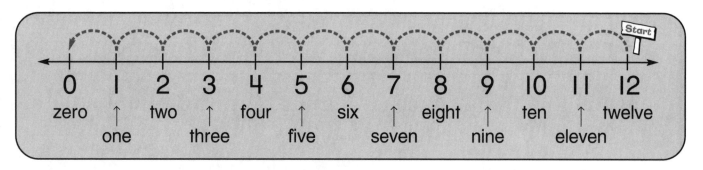

Count back. Write the missing numbers.

I.

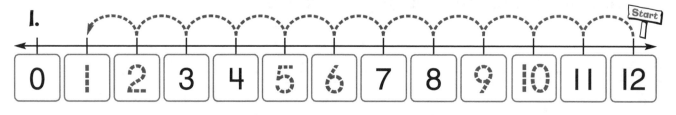

| 0 | 1 | 2 | 3 | 4 | 5 | 6 | 7 | 8 | 9 | 10 | 11 | 12 |

2.

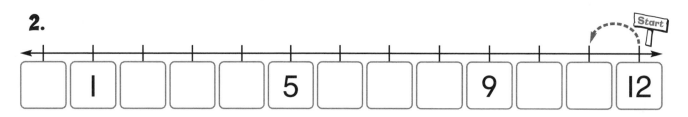

| | 1 | | | | 5 | | | | 9 | | | 12 |

3.

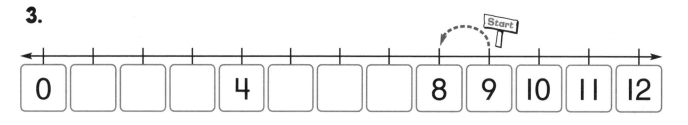

| 0 | | | | 4 | | | | 8 | 9 | 10 | 11 | 12 |

4.

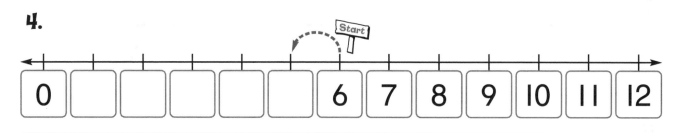

| 0 | | | | | | 6 | 7 | 8 | 9 | 10 | 11 | 12 |

5.

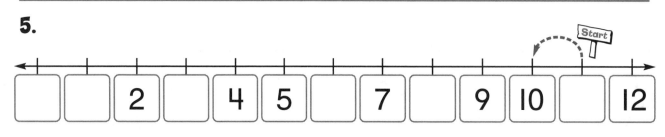

| | | 2 | | 4 | 5 | | 7 | | 9 | 10 | | 12 |

Use with Lesson 9, text pages 21–22.

Before, Between, After

Name _____

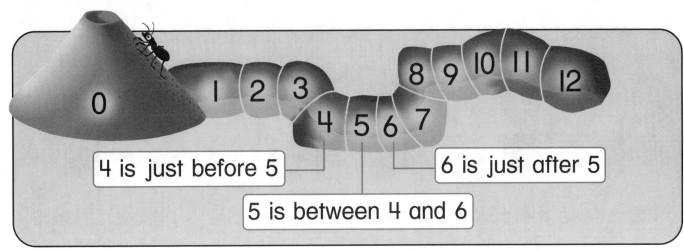

4 is just before 5

6 is just after 5

5 is between 4 and 6

1. Write the number that comes just before.

_4_ , 5   ___ , 4   ___ , 3   ___ , 8

___ , 2   ___ , 9   ___ , 12   ___ , 10

___ , 6   ___ , 11   ___ , 1   ___ , 7

2. Write the number that comes just after.

8, _9_   1, ___   9, ___   3, ___

5, ___   7, ___   10, ___   0, ___

11, ___   4, ___   2, ___   6, ___

3. Write the number that comes between.

8, _9_ , 10   7, ___ , 9   1, ___ , 3   5, ___ , 7

0, ___ , 2   6, ___ , 8   2, ___ , 4   3, ___ , 5

Use with Lesson 10, text pages 23–24.

nine **9**

Compare

Name _____

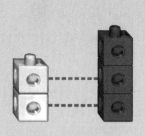 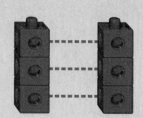 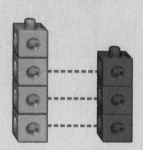

2 is less than 3	3 is equal to 3	4 is greater than 3
2 < 3	3 = 3	4 > 3

Write <, =, or >.

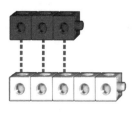 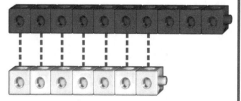 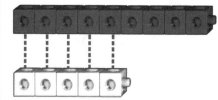

1. 3 (<) 5

2. 10 ◯ 7

3. 9 ◯ 5

4. 8 ◯ 12

5. 6 ◯ 10

6. 8 ◯ 8

7. 9 ◯ 9

8. 11 ◯ 9

9. 6 ◯ 3

10. twelve ◯ ten

11. seven ◯ eight

12. nine ◯ eleven

13. eight ◯ six

Use with Lesson 11, text pages 25–26.

Ordinals 1st Through 10th

Name _____

first	second	third	fourth	fifth
1st	2nd	3rd	4th	5th

1. Circle the position of each bug.

	(2nd)	7th	3rd
	2nd	5th	3rd
	4th	1st	10th
	9th	8th	4th
	2nd	10th	6th

2. Color the box. Start at the left.

tenth

eighth

seventh

ninth

sixth

Ordinals: From Top or Bottom

Name _____

Look at the bugs on the tree.
Write the ordinal number for each bug.

1.

2.

3.

4.

5.

6.

7.

8.

9.

10.

10th
tenth

9th
ninth

8th
eighth

7th
seventh

6th
sixth

5th
fifth

4th
fourth

3rd
third

2nd
second

1st
first

     Use with Lesson 13, text pages 31–32.

Problem-Solving Strategy:
Act It Out

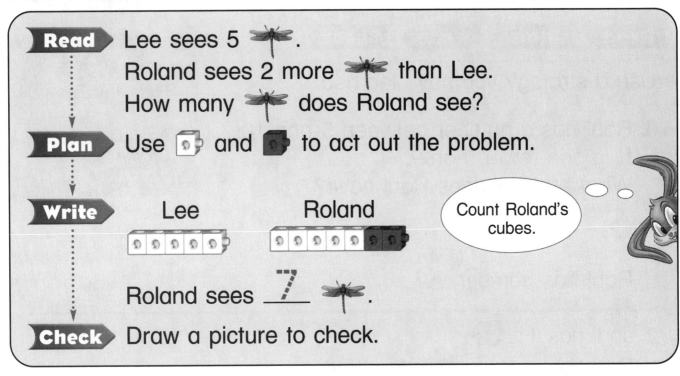

Read Lee sees 5 🦟.
Roland sees 2 more 🦟 than Lee.
How many 🦟 does Roland see?

Plan Use 🔲 and ⬛ to act out the problem.

Write Lee   Roland

Count Roland's cubes.

Roland sees ___7___ 🦟.

Check Draw a picture to check.

Act it out.

1. Paula finds 7 🦋.
   Ricky finds one fewer 🦋 than Paula.
   How many 🦋 does Ricky find?   Ricky finds ____ .

2. Iris catches 3 🐛.
   Fred catches 3 more 🐛 than Iris.
   How many 🐛 does Fred catch?   Fred catches ____ .

3. Bobby is fifth in line.
   Mari is tenth in line.
   How many children are between them?   ____ children

4. Juan draws 12 🐞.
   Mary draws 2 fewer 🐞 than Juan.
   How many 🐞 does Mary draw?   Mary draws ____ .

Problem-Solving Applications: Mixed Strategies

Name _____

Read ❯ **Plan** ❯ **Write** ❯ **Check**

Strategy File

Act It Out
Draw a Picture

Use a strategy you have learned.

1. Raul has a number between 5 and 10.
It is one fewer than 9.
What number does Raul have?

6, 7, 8, 9

Raul has number _8_.

2. Jodi has 11 .
Rob has 1 more than Jodi.
How many does Rob have?

Rob has ____ .

3. Saul is third in line.
Enid is last in line.
There are 3 children between them.
What position is Enid in line?

_____

Enid is _____ in line.

4. Jed caught 3 .
Sally caught 1 more than Jed.
How many did Sally catch?

Sally caught ____ .

Use with Lesson 15, text pages 35–36.

Understanding Addition

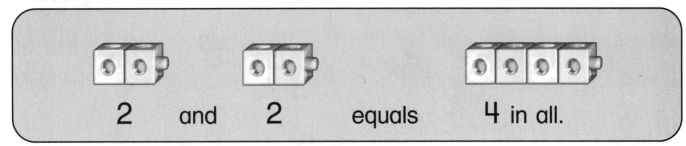

2 and **2** equals **4** in all.

Join  to model each addition story.
Write the numbers.

1.

___3___ 🐟 and ___2___ 🐟 equals ___5___ in all.

2.

___ 🦎 and ___ 🦎 equals ___ in all.

3.

___ 🐰 and ___ 🐰 equals ___ in all.

4.

___ 🦆 and ___ 🦆 equals ___ in all.

Addition Sentences

$$3 + 2 = 5$$
plus   equals

3 + 2 = 5 is an addition sentence .

Add. Write each addition sentence.

1.

___4___ + ___2___ = ___6___

2.

___ + ___ = ___

3.

___ + ___ = ___

4.

___ + ___ = ___

5.

___ + ___ = ___

6.

___ + ___ = ___

7.

___ + ___ = ___

8.

___ + ___ = ___

Use with Lesson 2, text pages 53–54.

Sums Through 6

You can write an addition fact in two ways.

$$\begin{array}{r} 3 \\ +\ 1 \\ \hline 4 \end{array}$$ addend
addend
sum

$$3 + 1 = 4$$

addend   addend   sum

Add.

1.

$\underline{3} + \underline{2} = \underline{5}$

2.

$0 + 4 = \underline{}$

3.

$1 + 2 = \underline{}$

4.

$1 + 1 = \underline{}$

5.

$$\begin{array}{r} 0 \\ +\ 2 \\ \hline 2 \end{array}$$

6.

$$\begin{array}{r} \\ +\ \\ \hline \end{array}$$

7.

$$\begin{array}{r} \\ +\ \\ \hline \end{array}$$

8.

$3 + 3 = \underline{}$

9.

$2 + 4 = \underline{}$

Related Addition Facts

Change the order of the addends and get the same sum.

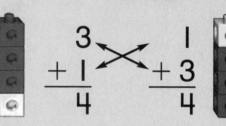

Horizontal	Vertical

$$3 + 1 = 4$$
$$1 + 3 = 4$$

$$+\begin{array}{r}3\\1\\\hline4\end{array} \qquad +\begin{array}{r}1\\3\\\hline4\end{array}$$

Add. Write the related addition fact.

1.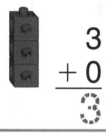

$$+\begin{array}{r}3\\0\\\hline3\end{array} \qquad +\begin{array}{r}0\\3\\\hline3\end{array}$$

2.

$$+\begin{array}{r}5\\1\\\hline\end{array} \qquad +\begin{array}{r}\\\\\hline\end{array}$$

3.

$$+\begin{array}{r}1\\2\\\hline\end{array} \qquad +\begin{array}{r}\\\\\hline\end{array}$$

4.

$$+\begin{array}{r}0\\6\\\hline\end{array} \qquad +\begin{array}{r}\\\\\hline\end{array}$$

5.

$$+\begin{array}{r}0\\4\\\hline\end{array} \qquad +\begin{array}{r}\\\\\hline\end{array}$$

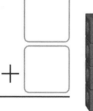

6.

$$+\begin{array}{r}2\\3\\\hline\end{array} \qquad +\begin{array}{r}\\\\\hline\end{array}$$

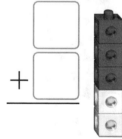

7.

$$1 + 4 = \underline{\hphantom{0}}$$

$$\underline{\hphantom{0}} + \underline{\hphantom{0}} = \underline{\hphantom{0}}$$

8.

$$3 + 2 = \underline{\hphantom{0}}$$

$$\underline{\hphantom{0}} + \underline{\hphantom{0}} = \underline{\hphantom{0}}$$

Use with Lesson 4, text pages 57–58.

Sums of 7 and 8

Name _____

$$6 + 2 = 8$$
part + part = whole

$$\begin{array}{r} 3 \\ +\,4 \\ \hline 7 \end{array}$$

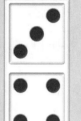

Find the sum. Draw and count to check.

1.
$$\begin{array}{r} 4 \\ +\,3 \\ \hline 7 \end{array}$$

2.
$$\begin{array}{r} 4 \\ +\,4 \\ \hline \end{array}$$

3.
$$\begin{array}{r} 1 \\ +\,7 \\ \hline \end{array}$$

4.
$$\begin{array}{r} 3 \\ +\,5 \\ \hline \end{array}$$

5.
$$\begin{array}{r} 2 \\ +\,5 \\ \hline \end{array}$$

6.
$$\begin{array}{r} 5 \\ +\,3 \\ \hline \end{array}$$

7. $8 + 0 = \underline{8}$

8. $1 + 6 = \underline{}$

9. $5 + 2 = \underline{}$

10. $3 + 4 = \underline{}$

11. $2 + 6 = \underline{}$

12. $6 + 1 = \underline{}$

Sums of 9 and 10

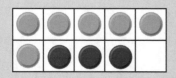
$$\begin{array}{r} 6 \\ + 3 \\ \hline 9 \end{array}$$

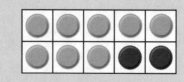
$$\begin{array}{r} 8 \\ + 2 \\ \hline 10 \end{array}$$

Draw ⬤ for the second addend.
Write the sum.

1.

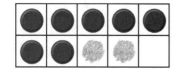 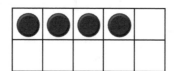 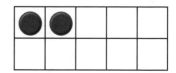

$7 + 2 = \underline{9}$ | $4 + 6 = \underline{}$ | $2 + 8 = \underline{}$

2.

 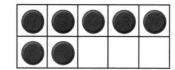 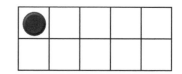

$1 + 8 = \underline{}$ | $7 + 3 = \underline{}$ | $1 + 9 = \underline{}$

Find the sum. Use a ▦ and ⬤ to check.

3.
$$\begin{array}{r} 5 \\ + 4 \\ \hline 9 \end{array} \qquad \begin{array}{r} 2 \\ + 7 \\ \hline \end{array} \qquad \begin{array}{r} 4 \\ + 5 \\ \hline \end{array} \qquad \begin{array}{r} 5 \\ + 5 \\ \hline \end{array} \qquad \begin{array}{r} 3 \\ + 6 \\ \hline \end{array} \qquad \begin{array}{r} 8 \\ + 1 \\ \hline \end{array}$$

4. $9 + 0 = \underline{}$ | $8 + 2 = \underline{}$ | $3 + 7 = \underline{}$

5. $6 + 4 = \underline{}$ | $7 + 3 = \underline{}$ | $6 + 3 = \underline{}$

6. $9 + 1 = \underline{}$ | $2 + 7 = \underline{}$ | $8 + 1 = \underline{}$

Use with Lesson 6, text pages 61–62.

Sums of 11 and 12

$$5 + 6 = 11$$

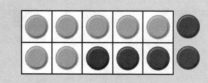
$$7 + 5 = 12$$

Find the sum.

1.

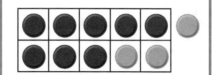

$6 + 6 = \underline{12}$ | $8 + 3 = \underline{}$ | $4 + 8 = \underline{}$

2.

 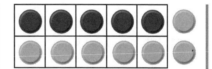 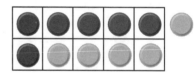

$9 + 2 = \underline{}$ | $5 + 7 = \underline{}$ | $6 + 5 = \underline{}$

Find the sum. Use a ▦ and ● to check.

3.
$$\begin{array}{c} 4 \\ +8 \\ \hline 12 \end{array} \quad \begin{array}{c} 4 \\ +7 \\ \hline \end{array} \quad \begin{array}{c} 3 \\ +9 \\ \hline \end{array} \quad \begin{array}{c} 9 \\ +2 \\ \hline \end{array} \quad \begin{array}{c} 5 \\ +7 \\ \hline \end{array} \quad \begin{array}{c} 2 \\ +9 \\ \hline \end{array}$$

4. $8 + 4 = \underline{}$ | $6 + 5 = \underline{}$ | $7 + 4 = \underline{}$

5. $3 + 8 = \underline{}$ | $7 + 5 = \underline{}$ | $6 + 6 = \underline{}$

6. $9 + 3 = \underline{}$ | $5 + 6 = \underline{}$ | $9 + 2 = \underline{}$

7. $4 + 7 = \underline{}$ | $5 + 7 = \underline{}$ | $3 + 9 = \underline{}$

Other Names for Numbers

Name _____

5 = 3 + 2   5 = 2 + 3   5 = 1 + 4

Write two ways to show each number.

1.

5 = ___ + ___

5 = ___ + ___

2.

10 = ___ + ___

10 = ___ + ___

3.

8 = ___ + ___

8 = ___ + ___

4.

3 = ___ + ___

3 = ___ + ___

5.

9 = ___ + ___

9 = ___ + ___

6.

12 = ___ + ___

12 = ___ + ___

Number-Line Addition

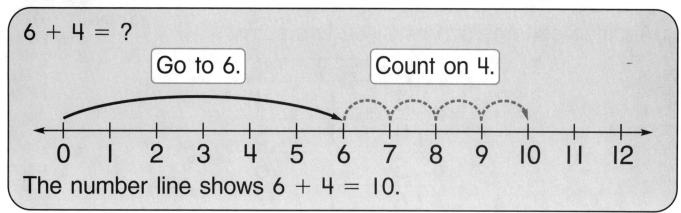

6 + 4 = ?

Go to 6.   Count on 4.

0 1 2 3 4 5 6 7 8 9 10 11 12

The number line shows 6 + 4 = 10.

Write the addition sentence shown for each number line.

1.

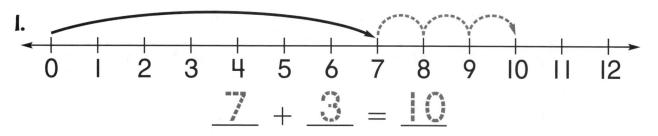

0 1 2 3 4 5 6 7 8 9 10 11 12

$\underline{7} + \underline{3} = \underline{10}$

2.

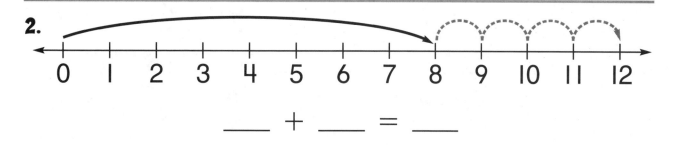

0 1 2 3 4 5 6 7 8 9 10 11 12

___ + ___ = ___

3.

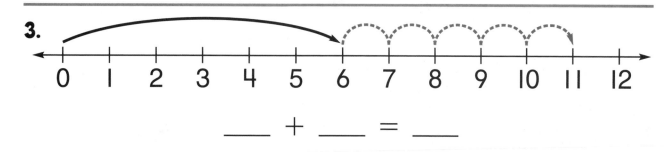

0 1 2 3 4 5 6 7 8 9 10 11 12

___ + ___ = ___

4.

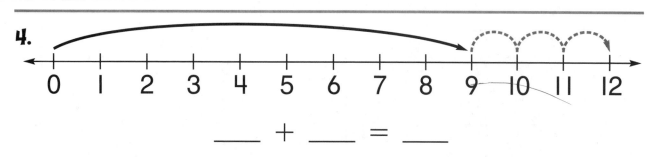

0 1 2 3 4 5 6 7 8 9 10 11 12

___ + ___ = ___

Add: Use Patterns

Name _____

Addition patterns can help you find sums.

Addend	Addend	Sum
3	1	4
4	1	5
5	1	6
6	1	7

Look for a pattern. Fill in the addition chart.

1.

Addend	Addend	Sum
4	0	4
4	1	
4	2	
4	3	

2.

Addend	Addend	Sum
5	2	
4	2	
3	2	
2	2	

3.

Addend	Addend	Sum
4	0	4
5	0	5
6	0	6
	0	7

4.

Addend	Addend	Sum
3	3	
3	2	
3	1	
3		

5.

Addend	Addend	Sum
6	6	
6	5	
6	4	
	3	

6.

Addend	Addend	Sum
0	4	
1	4	
2	4	
	4	

Use with Lesson 11, text pages 73–74.

Doubles

 $\begin{array}{r} 3 \text{ addend} \\ + 3 \text{ addend} \\ \hline 6 \text{ sum} \end{array}$

3 + 3 = 6 is a doubles fact.

Write the doubles fact.

1.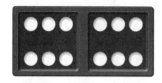

$\underline{6} + \underline{6} = \underline{12}$

2.

___ + ___ = ___

3.

___ + ___ = ___

4.

___ + ___ = ___

5.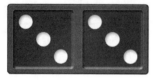

___ + ___ = ___

6.

___ + ___ = ___

Find the sum.

7. $\begin{array}{r} 5 \\ + 5 \\ \hline \end{array}$ **8.** $\begin{array}{r} 3 \\ + 3 \\ \hline \end{array}$ **9.** $\begin{array}{r} 2 \\ + 2 \\ \hline \end{array}$ **10.** $\begin{array}{r} 1 \\ + 1 \\ \hline \end{array}$ **11.** $\begin{array}{r} 4 \\ + 4 \\ \hline \end{array}$ **12.** $\begin{array}{r} 6 \\ + 6 \\ \hline \end{array}$

Use with Lesson 12, text pages 75–76.

Doubles Plus 1

Name _____

Use a doubles fact to add 1 + 2.

1 + 2 is 1 more than 1 + 1.

$1 + 1 = 2$ $1 + 2 = 3$

Find the sum.

1.

$3 + 3 = \underline{6}$ $3 + 4 = \underline{\quad}$

2.

$5 + 5 = \underline{\quad}$ $5 + 6 = \underline{\quad}$

3. $2 + 2 = \underline{\quad}$ $2 + 3 = \underline{\quad}$

4. $1 + 1 = \underline{\quad}$ $1 + 2 = \underline{\quad}$

5.
$$\begin{array}{r} 4 \\ +4 \\ \hline \end{array} \qquad \begin{array}{r} 4 \\ +5 \\ \hline \end{array}$$

6.
$$\begin{array}{r} 1 \\ +1 \\ \hline \end{array} \qquad \begin{array}{r} 1 \\ +2 \\ \hline \end{array}$$

7.
$$\begin{array}{r} 2 \\ +2 \\ \hline \end{array} \qquad \begin{array}{r} 2 \\ +3 \\ \hline \end{array}$$

8.
$$\begin{array}{r} 3 \\ +3 \\ \hline \end{array} \qquad \begin{array}{r} 3 \\ +4 \\ \hline \end{array}$$

9.
$$\begin{array}{r} 0 \\ +0 \\ \hline \end{array} \qquad \begin{array}{r} 0 \\ +1 \\ \hline \end{array}$$

10.
$$\begin{array}{r} 5 \\ +5 \\ \hline \end{array} \qquad \begin{array}{r} 5 \\ +6 \\ \hline \end{array}$$

Add Three Numbers

To add three numbers, group two addends.
Then add the third addend.

Add down.	**Add up.**

$$\begin{array}{c} \boxed{\begin{array}{c}2\\4\end{array}} \rightarrow 6 \\ +3 \quad +3 \\ \hline \quad\quad 9 \end{array}$$

$$\begin{array}{c} 2 \\ \boxed{\begin{array}{c}4\\3\end{array}} \rightarrow \begin{array}{c}2\\+7\end{array} \\ +3 \quad \hline \\ \quad\quad 9 \end{array}$$

Add left to right.

$$\boxed{2 + 4} + 3 = ?$$
$$6 \quad + 3 = 9$$

Add right to left.

$$2 + \boxed{4 + 3} = ?$$
$$2 + \quad 7 \quad = 9$$

Add. You can use ▦ to help.

1.
$$\begin{array}{c} 5 \\ \boxed{\begin{array}{c}3\\3\end{array}} \rightarrow \begin{array}{c}5\\+\boxed{6}\end{array} \\ + \end{array}$$

2.
$$\boxed{\begin{array}{c}3\\1\end{array}} \rightarrow \square \\ +8 \quad +8$$

3.
$$\boxed{\begin{array}{c}2\\2\end{array}} \rightarrow \square \\ +5 \quad +5$$

4.
$$\begin{array}{c}1\\\boxed{\begin{array}{c}1\\9\end{array}}\end{array} \rightarrow \begin{array}{c}1\\+\square\end{array}$$

5.
$$\boxed{\begin{array}{c}3\\2\end{array}} \rightarrow \square \\ +7 \quad +7$$

6.
$$\begin{array}{c}2\\\boxed{\begin{array}{c}1\\7\end{array}}\end{array} \rightarrow \begin{array}{c}2\\+\square\end{array}$$

7.
$$\begin{array}{c}3\\\boxed{\begin{array}{c}1\\4\end{array}}\end{array} \rightarrow \begin{array}{c}3\\+\square\end{array}$$

8.
$$\begin{array}{c}3\\\boxed{\begin{array}{c}4\\4\end{array}}\end{array} \rightarrow \begin{array}{c}3\\+\square\end{array}$$

9. $\boxed{2 + 5} + 2 = ?$

$$\underline{\quad} + 2 = \underline{\quad}$$

10. $2 + \boxed{2 + 7} = ?$

$$2 + \underline{\quad} = \underline{\quad}$$

Addition Strategies with Three Addends

Name _____

Find the sum.
Circle the addends you add first.

1. $\boxed{1 + 1} + 6 = ?$

$\underline{2} + \underline{6} = \underline{8}$

2. $5 + 3 + 2 = ?$

$\underline{} + \underline{} = \underline{}$

3. $7 + 2 + 2 = ?$

$\underline{} + \underline{} = \underline{}$

4. $6 + 2 + 3 = ?$

$\underline{} + \underline{} = \underline{}$

5. $3 + 4 + 2 = ?$

$\underline{} + \underline{} = \underline{}$

6. $3 + 5 + 4 = ?$

$\underline{} + \underline{} = \underline{}$

7. $1 + 1 + 7 = ?$

$\underline{} + \underline{} = \underline{}$

8. $4 + 2 + 4 = ?$

$\underline{} + \underline{} = \underline{}$

9.
$\begin{array}{r} \boxed{5} \\ 1 \\ + \boxed{5} \\ \hline 11 \end{array}$
$\begin{array}{r} \boxed{10} \\ \boxed{1} \\ + \\ \hline \end{array}$

10.
$\begin{array}{r} 4 \\ 5 \\ + 3 \\ \hline \end{array}$
$+ \boxed{}$

11.
$\begin{array}{r} 8 \\ 1 \\ + 1 \\ \hline \end{array}$
$+ \boxed{}$

12.
$\begin{array}{r} 3 \\ 3 \\ + 6 \\ \hline \end{array}$
$+ \boxed{}$

Use with Lesson 16, text pages 85–86.

Problem-Solving Strategy:
Write a Number Sentence

Name _____

Read ▸ Archie has 2 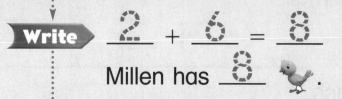.
Millen has 6 more 🐦 than Archie.
How many 🐦 does Millen have?

Plan ▸ Write a number sentence.

Write ▸ $\underline{2} + \underline{6} = \underline{8}$
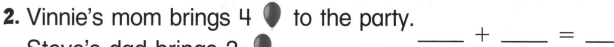
Millen has $\underline{8}$ 🐦.

Check ▸ Change the order of the addends to check.

---

1. Buddy buys 7 🐢.
Phyllis buys 2 more 🐢 than Buddy.   ___ + ___ = ___

How many 🐢 does Phyllis buy?   Phyllis buys ___ 🐢.

---

2. Vinnie's mom brings 4 🎈 to the party.
Steve's dad brings 3 🎈.   ___ + ___ = ___

How many 🎈 do they bring in all?   They bring ___ 🎈.

---

3. Billy picks 2 🌼 from his garden. His   ___ + ___ = ___
sister Del picks 2 more 🌼 than Billy.

How many 🌼 does Del pick?   Del picks ___ 🌼.

---

4. Erma puts 5 🌶 in her chili.
Paul puts only 1 🌶 in his chili.   ___ + ___ = ___

How many 🌶 do they use in all?   They use ___ 🌶.

Use with Lesson 17, text pages 87–88.   twenty-nine **29**

Problem-Solving Applications: Mixed Strategies

Name _____

Read ▶ **Plan** ▶ **Write** ▶ **Check**

Use a strategy you have learned.

Strategy File

Act It Out
Draw a Picture
Write a Number Sentence

I. At the zoo, one cage has 2 .
Another cage has 5 .
How many are there in all?

There are __7__ .

$$2 + 5 = 7$$

2. Kim sees 6 on a beach.
Two more join them.
How many are there in all?

There are ____ .

3. Ellis has 7 🐟.
His brother Percy has I 🐱.
How many animals do they have in all?

They have ____ animals in all.

4. On Monday, Ann sees 3 🐦.
On Tuesday, Todd sees as many 🐦 as Ann saw.
How many birds do they see in all?

They see ____ birds in all.

5. Ray and Dora each catch 2 🐢.
Polly catches I 🐢.
How many do they catch in all?

They catch ____ 🐢 in all.

Use with Lesson 18, text pages 89–90.

Understanding Subtraction

6 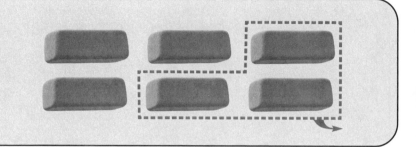 in all.

Take away 3 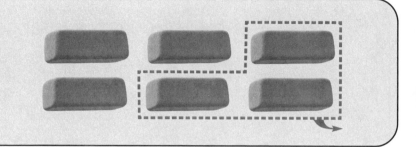 .

3 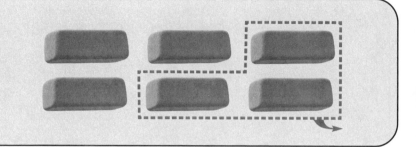 left.

Use to model each subtraction story.
Write the numbers.

1. __4__  in all.

Take away __1__ .

__3__  left.

2. ____ in all.

Take away ____ .

____ left.

3. ____ in all.

Take away ____  .

____ left.

4. ____  in all.

Take away ____  .

____  left.

Subtraction Sentences

5 − 2 = 3 is a subtraction sentence.

$$5 \underset{\text{minus}}{\underset{\uparrow}{-}} 2 \underset{\text{equals}}{\underset{\uparrow}{=}} 3$$

A subtraction sentence uses the symbols − and =.

Subtract. Write each subtraction sentence.

1.

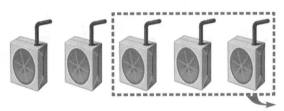

$$\underline{5} - \underline{3} = \underline{}$$

2.

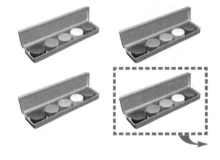

$$\underline{} - \underline{} = \underline{}$$

3.

$$\underline{} - \underline{} = \underline{}$$

4.

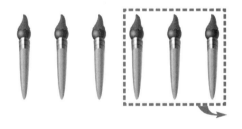

$$\underline{} - \underline{} = \underline{}$$

5.

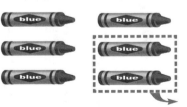

$$\underline{} - \underline{} = \underline{}$$

6.

$$\underline{} - \underline{} = \underline{}$$

Use with Lesson 2, text pages 103–104.

Subtract from 6 or Less

You can write subtraction facts in two ways.

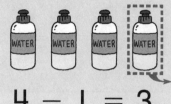

$$4$$
$$\underline{-\ 1}$$
$$3 \text{ difference}$$

$$4 - 1 = 3$$
difference ← the number left

Find the difference.

1.

$$6$$
$$\underline{-\ 1}$$
$$5$$

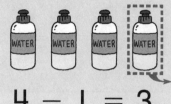

$$6 - 1 = \underline{5}$$

2.

$$3$$
$$\underline{-\ 3}$$

$$3 - 3 = \underline{}$$

3.

$$5$$
$$\underline{-\ 1}$$

$$5 - 1 = \underline{}$$

4.

$$3$$
$$\underline{-\ 2}$$

$$3 - 2 = \underline{}$$

5. $\quad 4 - 4 = \underline{0}$

6. $\quad 5 - 0 = \underline{}$

7. $\quad 3 - 1 = \underline{}$

8. $\quad 6 - 3 = \underline{}$

9. $\quad 6 - 5 = \underline{}$

10. $\quad 4 - 2 = \underline{}$

11.
$$3$$
$$\underline{-\ 0}$$

12.
$$6$$
$$\underline{-\ 2}$$

13.
$$2$$
$$\underline{-\ 1}$$

14.
$$5$$
$$\underline{-\ 3}$$

15.
$$6$$
$$\underline{-\ 4}$$

16.
$$4$$
$$\underline{-\ 3}$$

All or Zero

Name _____

$$5 - 5 = 0 \qquad 5 - 0 = 5 \qquad 5 + 0 = 5$$

Add or subtract.

1.	2.	3.	4.	5.
4 − 4 0	3 + 0	2 − 0	1 − 1	6 − 0

6.	7.	8.	9.	10.
1 + 0	2 + 0	4 − 0	3 − 3	6 + 0

11.	12.	13.	14.	15.
4 + 0	5 + 0	6 − 6	0 + 5	3 − 0

16. $2 - 2 =$ _____   17. $1 - 0 =$ _____

Problem Solving Solve. Use a problem-solving strategy.

18. Jean brought 3 ▬ to the test. None of them got lost. How many ▬ does she have?

_____ − _____ = _____

19. Cissy has 6 ▢ on her desk. She gives them all to Rick. How many ▢ does she have left?

_____ − _____ = _____

Use with Lesson 4, text pages 107–108.

Subtract from 7 and 8

Name _____

Ed has 7 🍎. Three are red and some are green. How many apples are not red?

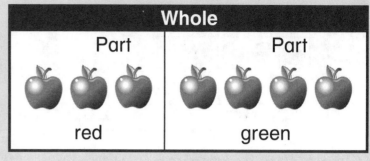

	Whole	
Part		Part
🍎🍎🍎		🍎🍎🍎🍎
red		green

$$7 \quad - \quad 3 \quad = \quad 4$$

whole − part = part

$$\begin{array}{r} 7 \\ -3 \\ \hline 4 \end{array} \begin{array}{l} \text{whole} \\ \text{part} \\ \text{part} \end{array}$$

4 🍎 are not red.

Subtract.

1.
$$\begin{array}{r} 7 \\ -1 \\ \hline 6 \end{array} \qquad \begin{array}{r} 8 \\ -4 \\ \hline \end{array} \qquad \begin{array}{r} 7 \\ -2 \\ \hline \end{array} \qquad \begin{array}{r} 8 \\ -2 \\ \hline \end{array} \qquad \begin{array}{r} 7 \\ -4 \\ \hline \end{array} \qquad \begin{array}{r} 8 \\ -7 \\ \hline \end{array}$$

2.
$$\begin{array}{r} 8 \\ -8 \\ \hline \end{array} \qquad \begin{array}{r} 7 \\ -7 \\ \hline \end{array} \qquad \begin{array}{r} 7 \\ -5 \\ \hline \end{array} \qquad \begin{array}{r} 8 \\ -3 \\ \hline \end{array} \qquad \begin{array}{r} 8 \\ -5 \\ \hline \end{array} \qquad \begin{array}{r} 8 \\ -0 \\ \hline \end{array}$$

3.
$$\begin{array}{r} 7 \\ -3 \\ \hline \end{array} \qquad \begin{array}{r} 8 \\ -6 \\ \hline \end{array} \qquad \begin{array}{r} 7 \\ -6 \\ \hline \end{array} \qquad \begin{array}{r} 7 \\ -0 \\ \hline \end{array} \qquad \begin{array}{r} 8 \\ -1 \\ \hline \end{array} \qquad \begin{array}{r} 8 \\ -4 \\ \hline \end{array}$$

4. $7 - 7 = \underline{0}$ $7 - 1 = \underline{}$ $8 - 5 = \underline{}$

5. $8 - 4 = \underline{}$ $7 - 4 = \underline{}$ $7 - 2 = \underline{}$

Subtract from 9 and 10

Name _____

$$9 - 2 = 7 \qquad 10 - 4 = 6$$

Circle the part taken away. Write the difference.

1.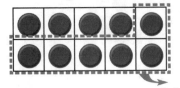

$$10 - 6 = \underline{4}$$

2.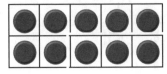

$$10 - 3 = \underline{}$$

3.

$$9 - 8 = \underline{}$$

4.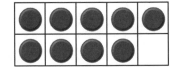

$$9 - 0 = \underline{}$$

Subtract. Use a ▦ and ● to help.

5.
$$\begin{array}{r} 9 \\ -4 \\ \hline 5 \end{array} \qquad \begin{array}{r} 10 \\ -5 \\ \hline \end{array} \qquad \begin{array}{r} 9 \\ -1 \\ \hline \end{array} \qquad \begin{array}{r} 10 \\ -7 \\ \hline \end{array} \qquad \begin{array}{r} 9 \\ -3 \\ \hline \end{array} \qquad \begin{array}{r} 10 \\ -8 \\ \hline \end{array}$$

6.
$$\begin{array}{r} 10 \\ -6 \\ \hline \end{array} \qquad \begin{array}{r} 9 \\ -6 \\ \hline \end{array} \qquad \begin{array}{r} 10 \\ -1 \\ \hline \end{array} \qquad \begin{array}{r} 9 \\ -2 \\ \hline \end{array} \qquad \begin{array}{r} 10 \\ -0 \\ \hline \end{array} \qquad \begin{array}{r} 9 \\ -5 \\ \hline \end{array}$$

7.
$$\begin{array}{r} 10 \\ -9 \\ \hline \end{array} \qquad \begin{array}{r} 9 \\ -7 \\ \hline \end{array} \qquad \begin{array}{r} 10 \\ -10 \\ \hline \end{array} \qquad \begin{array}{r} 10 \\ -2 \\ \hline \end{array} \qquad \begin{array}{r} 9 \\ -0 \\ \hline \end{array} \qquad \begin{array}{r} 9 \\ -9 \\ \hline \end{array}$$

Use with Lesson 6, text pages 111–112.

Subtract from 11 and 12

 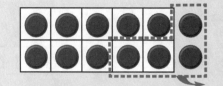

$$11 - 4 = 7 \qquad 12 - 4 = 8$$

Write the difference.

1.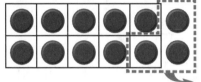

$$12 - 3 = \underline{9}$$

2.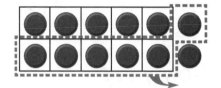

$$12 - 6 = \underline{}$$

Subtract. Use a ▦ and ● to help.

3.
$$\begin{array}{c} 12 \\ -\ 5 \\ \hline 7 \end{array} \qquad \begin{array}{c} 11 \\ -\ 4 \\ \hline \end{array} \qquad \begin{array}{c} 11 \\ -\ 7 \\ \hline \end{array} \qquad \begin{array}{c} 11 \\ -\ 5 \\ \hline \end{array} \qquad \begin{array}{c} 12 \\ -\ 8 \\ \hline \end{array} \qquad \begin{array}{c} 11 \\ -\ 6 \\ \hline \end{array}$$

4.
$$\begin{array}{c} 12 \\ -\ 9 \\ \hline \end{array} \qquad \begin{array}{c} 12 \\ -\ 7 \\ \hline \end{array} \qquad \begin{array}{c} 11 \\ -\ 2 \\ \hline \end{array} \qquad \begin{array}{c} 11 \\ -\ 8 \\ \hline \end{array} \qquad \begin{array}{c} 11 \\ -\ 3 \\ \hline \end{array} \qquad \begin{array}{c} 12 \\ -\ 6 \\ \hline \end{array}$$

5.
$$\begin{array}{c} 12 \\ -\ 3 \\ \hline \end{array} \qquad \begin{array}{c} 11 \\ -\ 3 \\ \hline \end{array} \qquad \begin{array}{c} 11 \\ -\ 5 \\ \hline \end{array} \qquad \begin{array}{c} 12 \\ -\ 8 \\ \hline \end{array} \qquad \begin{array}{c} 11 \\ -\ 4 \\ \hline \end{array} \qquad \begin{array}{c} 12 \\ -\ 5 \\ \hline \end{array}$$

6.
$$\begin{array}{c} 11 \\ -\ 9 \\ \hline \end{array} \qquad \begin{array}{c} 12 \\ -\ 4 \\ \hline \end{array} \qquad \begin{array}{c} 11 \\ -\ 7 \\ \hline \end{array} \qquad \begin{array}{c} 12 \\ -\ 6 \\ \hline \end{array} \qquad \begin{array}{c} 11 \\ -\ 6 \\ \hline \end{array} \qquad \begin{array}{c} 11 \\ -\ 3 \\ \hline \end{array}$$

Number-Line Subtraction

Name _____

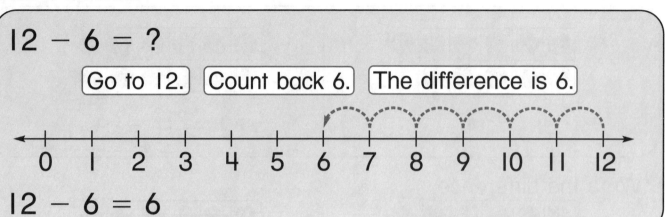

$12 - 6 = ?$

| Go to 12. | Count back 6. | The difference is 6. |

$12 - 6 = 6$

Show how you count back to subtract. Write the difference.

I. $11 - 9 = \underline{2}$

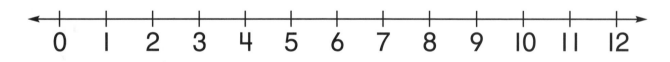

2. $12 - 3 = \underline{}$

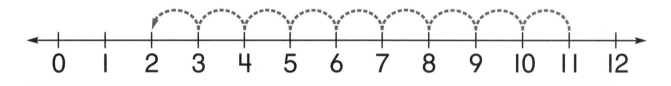

3. $11 - 3 = \underline{}$

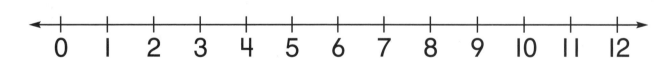

4. $8 - 6 = \underline{}$

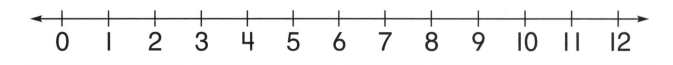

Use with Lesson 8, text pages 117–118.

Rules and Patterns

Name _____

Whole	Part Taken Away	Part Left
12	5	7
11	5	6
10	5	5

What is the pattern rule?

$12 - 5 = 7$
$11 - 5 = 6$
$10 - 5 = 5$

The pattern rule is $- 5$.

Fill in the subtraction chart. What is the pattern rule?

1.

Whole	Part Taken Away	Part Left
9	6	
8	6	
7	6	

The pattern rule is __6__.

2.

Whole	Part Taken Away	Part Left
6	3	
7	3	
8	3	

The pattern rule is _____.

3.

Whole	Part Taken Away	Part Left
8	7	
9	7	
10	7	

The pattern rule is _____.

4.

Whole	Part Taken Away	Part Left
7	2	
6	2	
5	2	

The pattern rule is _____.

5.

Whole	Part Taken Away	Part Left
4	1	
3	1	
2	1	

The pattern rule is _____.

6.

Whole	Part Taken Away	Part Left
8	0	
7	0	
6	0	

The pattern rule is _____.

Use with Lesson 9, text pages 119–120.

Related Subtraction Facts

Related subtraction facts have the same numbers.
They can be written two ways.

Horizontal

$7 - 3 = 4$

$7 - 4 = 3$

Vertical

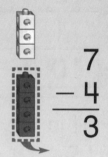

$$\begin{array}{r} 7 \\ -\ 3 \\ \hline 4 \end{array}$$

$$\begin{array}{r} 7 \\ -\ 4 \\ \hline 3 \end{array}$$

Subtract. Write the related subtraction fact.

1.
$$\begin{array}{r} 5 \\ -\ 1 \\ \hline 4 \end{array}$$
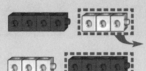
$$\begin{array}{r} -\ \\ \hline \end{array}$$

2.
$$\begin{array}{r} 11 \\ -\ 6 \\ \hline \end{array}$$
$$-\ \boxed{}$$

3.
$$\begin{array}{r} 9 \\ -\ 5 \\ \hline \end{array}$$
$$-\ \boxed{}$$

4.
$$\begin{array}{r} 10 \\ -\ 4 \\ \hline \end{array}$$
$$-\ \boxed{}$$

5.
$$\begin{array}{r} 12 \\ -\ 3 \\ \hline \end{array}$$
$$-\ \boxed{}$$

6.
$$\begin{array}{r} 7 \\ -\ 0 \\ \hline \end{array}$$
$$-\ \boxed{}$$

7.
$$\begin{array}{r} 3 \\ -\ 2 \\ \hline \end{array}$$
$$-\ \boxed{}$$

8.
$$\begin{array}{r} 11 \\ -\ 7 \\ \hline \end{array}$$
$$-\ \boxed{}$$

9. $8 - 6 = \underline{}$

$\underline{} - \underline{} = \underline{}$

10. $12 - 8 = \underline{}$

$\underline{} - \underline{} = \underline{}$

11. $7 - 5 = \underline{}$

$\underline{} - \underline{} = \underline{}$

12. $11 - 8 = \underline{}$

$\underline{} - \underline{} = \underline{}$

Use with Lesson 10, text pages 121–122.

Relate Addition and Subtraction

These are related addition and subtraction facts.
Both facts use the same numbers.

$$5 + 1 = 6 \qquad\qquad 6 - 1 = 5$$

Add. Write the related subtracton fact.

I.
$$2 + 3 = 5$$
$$5 - 3 = 2$$

2.
$$3 + 3 = \underline{}$$
$$\underline{} - \underline{} = \underline{}$$

3.
$$2 + 2 = \underline{}$$
$$\underline{} - \underline{} = \underline{}$$

4.
$$1 + 3 = \underline{}$$
$$\underline{} - \underline{} = \underline{}$$

5.
$$0 + 3 = \underline{}$$
$$\underline{} - \underline{} = \underline{}$$

6.
$$4 + 2 = \underline{}$$
$$\underline{} - \underline{} = \underline{}$$

7.
$$5 + 3 = \underline{}$$
$$\underline{} - \underline{} = \underline{}$$

8.
$$6 + 3 = \underline{}$$
$$\underline{} - \underline{} = \underline{}$$

9.
$$3 + 4 = \underline{}$$
$$\underline{} - \underline{} = \underline{}$$

10.
$$5 + 4 = \underline{}$$
$$\underline{} - \underline{} = \underline{}$$

Check by Adding

Name _____

> **Subtract.**
> $$6 - 3 = 3$$
>
> **Add the parts to check.**
> $$3 + 3 = 6$$

Subtract. Then add to check your answer.

I. $7 - 2 = 5$
$5 + 2 = 7$

2. $11 - 6 = \underline{\quad}$
$\underline{\quad} + \underline{\quad} = \underline{\quad}$

3. $8 - 4 = \underline{\quad}$
$\underline{\quad} + \underline{\quad} = \underline{\quad}$

4. $9 - 3 = \underline{\quad}$
$\underline{\quad} + \underline{\quad} = \underline{\quad}$

5.
$$\begin{array}{r} 10 \\ -\ 4 \\ \hline 6 \end{array} \quad + \begin{array}{|c|} \hline 6 \\ \hline 4 \\ \hline \end{array}$$

6.
$$\begin{array}{r} 11 \\ -\ 4 \\ \hline \end{array} \quad + \begin{array}{|c|} \hline \ \\ \hline \ \\ \hline \end{array}$$

7.
$$\begin{array}{r} 12 \\ -\ 4 \\ \hline \end{array} \quad + \begin{array}{|c|} \hline \ \\ \hline \ \\ \hline \end{array}$$

8.
$$\begin{array}{r} 11 \\ -\ 8 \\ \hline \end{array} \quad + \begin{array}{|c|} \hline \ \\ \hline \ \\ \hline \end{array}$$

9.
$$\begin{array}{r} 12 \\ -\ 7 \\ \hline \end{array} \quad + \begin{array}{|c|} \hline \ \\ \hline \ \\ \hline \end{array}$$

10.
$$\begin{array}{r} 10 \\ -\ 8 \\ \hline \end{array} \quad + \begin{array}{|c|} \hline \ \\ \hline \ \\ \hline \end{array}$$

II.
$$\begin{array}{r} 9 \\ -\ 5 \\ \hline \end{array} \quad + \begin{array}{|c|} \hline \ \\ \hline \ \\ \hline \end{array}$$

12.
$$\begin{array}{r} 10 \\ -\ 7 \\ \hline \end{array} \quad + \begin{array}{|c|} \hline \ \\ \hline \ \\ \hline \end{array}$$

13.
$$\begin{array}{r} 12 \\ 6 \\ \hline \end{array} \quad + \begin{array}{|c|} \hline \ \\ \hline \ \\ \hline \end{array}$$

Use with Lesson 12, text pages 125–126.

Fact Families

Name _____

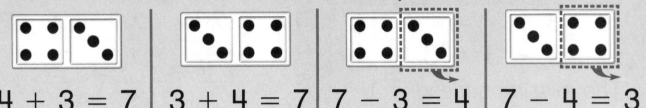

A fact family shows all the related facts for a set of numbers. This is the fact family for 3, 4, 7.

$$4 + 3 = 7 \mid 3 + 4 = 7 \mid 7 - 3 = 4 \mid 7 - 4 = 3$$

Write the fact families.

1.

$$2 + 4 = \underline{6}$$
$$\underline{} + \underline{} = \underline{}$$
$$\underline{} - \underline{} = \underline{}$$
$$\underline{} - \underline{} = \underline{}$$

2.

$$3 + 5 = \underline{}$$
$$\underline{} + \underline{} = \underline{}$$
$$\underline{} - \underline{} = \underline{}$$
$$\underline{} - \underline{} = \underline{}$$

3.

$$\begin{array}{r} 3 \\ + 8 \\ \hline \end{array} \quad +\square \quad -\square \quad -\square$$

4.

$$\begin{array}{r} 5 \\ + 7 \\ \hline \end{array} \quad +\square \quad -\square \quad -\square$$

5.

$$\begin{array}{r} 6 \\ + 3 \\ \hline \end{array} \quad +\square \quad -\square \quad -\square$$

6.

$$\begin{array}{r} 2 \\ + 6 \\ \hline \end{array} \quad +\square \quad -\square \quad -\square$$

Use with Lesson 13, text pages 127–128.

Find Missing Addends

Use a subtraction fact to find the missing addend.

$$3 + ? = 6$$
$$6 - 3 = 3$$

The missing addend is 3.

So $3 + 3 = 6$.

Use a subtraction fact to find the missing addend.

I. $7 + ? = 11$

$$\underline{11} - \underline{7} = \underline{4}$$

So $7 + \underline{4} = 11$.

2. $8 + ? = 10$

$$\underline{} - \underline{} = \underline{}$$

So $8 + \underline{} = 10$.

3. $? + 6 = 6$

$$\underline{} - \underline{} = \underline{}$$

So $\underline{} + 6 = 6$.

4. $5 + ? = 12$

$$\underline{} - \underline{} = \underline{}$$

So $5 + \underline{} = 12$.

5. $3 + ? = 8$

$$\underline{} - \underline{} = \underline{}$$

So $3 + \underline{} = 8$.

6. $2 + ? = 11$

$$\underline{} - \underline{} = \underline{}$$

So $2 + \underline{} = 11$.

7. $? + 2 = 9$

$$\underline{} - \underline{} = \underline{}$$

So $\underline{} + 2 = 9$.

8.
$$\begin{array}{r} ? \\ + 3 \\ \hline 4 \end{array} \qquad \begin{array}{r} 4 \\ - 3 \\ \hline \end{array} \qquad \begin{array}{r} \\ + 3 \\ \hline 4 \end{array}$$

9.
$$\begin{array}{r} 6 \\ + ? \\ \hline 10 \end{array} \qquad \begin{array}{r} \\ - \\ \hline \end{array} \qquad \begin{array}{r} 6 \\ + \\ \hline 10 \end{array}$$

Use with Lesson 14, text pages 131–132.

Subtract to Compare

Draw ◯ to compare. Then subtract to find the answer.

Rose has 9 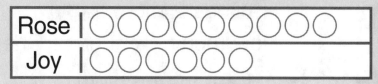 .
Joy has 6 .
Who has more?
How many more?

Rose	◯◯◯◯◯◯◯◯◯
Joy	◯◯◯◯◯◯

$$9 - 6 = 3$$

Rose has 3 more .

Draw ◯ to compare. Then subtract.

1. Alex bought 4 .
Tia bought 8 .
Who bought
fewer ?
How many fewer?

Alex	◯◯◯◯
Tia	◯◯◯◯◯◯◯◯

$$\underline{8} - \underline{4} = \underline{4}$$

__Alex__ bought __4__ fewer .

2. Ron has 4 .
Tom has 7 .
Who has
more ?
How many more?

Ron	
Tom	

___ − ___ = ___

_____ has ___ more .

3. Ted holds 6 .
Bryan holds 10 .
Who holds
more ?
How many more?

Ted	
Bryan	

___ − ___ = ___

_____ holds ___ more .

Problem-Solving Strategy: Choose the Operation

Name _____

Read ▶ Chen has 4 🍬.
He finds 2 more 🍬.
How many 🍬 does Chen have now?

Plan ▶ Act out the problem.
Choose: (add) subtract

🍬🍬🍬🍬   🍬🍬

Write ▶ __4__ (+) __2__ = __6__

Chen has __6__ 🍬 now.

Write a number sentence.

Check ▶ Change the order of the addends to check.

---

1. Paul has 7 ✏️.
He gives 3 ✏️ away.
How many ✏️ does Paul have now?

add   subtract

____ ◯ ____ = ____

Paul has ____ ✏️ now.

2. 6 🖍️ are on Tai's desk.
Tai puts 3 more 🖍️ there.
How many 🖍️ are on Tai's desk then?

add   subtract

____ ◯ ____ = ____

____ 🖍️ are on Tai's desk.

---

3. John finds 1 🖊️ in his desk and 5 🖊️ on the floor.
How many 🖊️ does John find in all?

add   subtract

____ ◯ ____ = ____

John finds ____ 🖊️.

4. Alma sees 9 🚩.
5 🚩 are taken away.
How many 🚩 are left?

add   subtract

____ ◯ ____ = ____

There are ____ 🚩 left.

Use with Lesson 18, text pages 139–140.

Problem-Solving Applications: Mixed Strategies

Name _____

Read ▸ **Plan** ▸ **Write** ▸ **Check**

Use a strategy you have learned.

Strategy File

Choose the Operation
Act It Out
Draw a Picture

1. Lisa ate 3 yesterday.
She ate 4 today.
How many did Lisa eat in all?

Lisa ate __7__ in all.

$$3 + 4 = 7$$

2. There are 9 on the closet shelf.
4 fall off the shelf.
How many are left?

There are ____ left.

3. Sandy wants to find 10 .
She found 8 yesterday.
How many more does she need to find?

Sandy needs to find ____ more .

4. Ben and Paula each buy 5 .
Karen buys 2 .
How many do they buy in all?

They buy ____ in all.

5. Josie is third in line in the lunch room.
Her friend Eva is 2 children behind Josie.
What position is Eva in line?

Eva is ____ in line.

Venn Diagrams

Name _____

You can use a Venn diagram to show how things are different and how they are alike.

These shapes are grey.   These shapes are large.

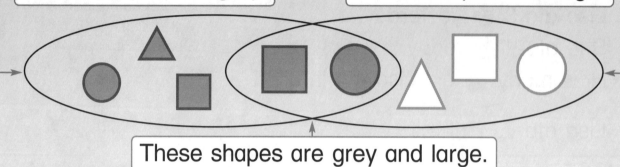

These shapes are grey and large.

Draw each shape inside the Venn diagram.

I.

These shapes are large.   These shapes are grey.

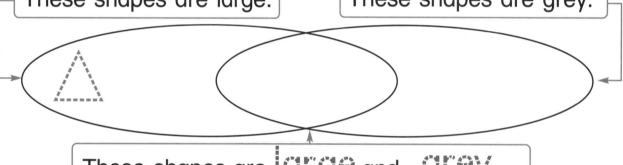

These shapes are large and grey .

2.

These circles are small.   These circles are white.

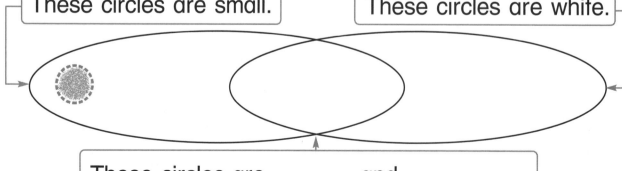

These circles are _____ and _____ .

Use with Lesson I, text pages 157–158.

Tally Charts

Tally the stickers.
Each | stands for 1.
Each |||| stands for 5.

Number of Stickers		
Sticker	Tally	Number
						5
					3
				2

Tally to show how many of each toy dinosaur.
X each dinosaur as you make each tally.

1.

Toy Dinosaurs		
Dinosaur	Tally	Number
	⋮	

___

2. How many dinosaurs did you tally in all?

____ ◯ ____ ◯ ____ = ____

3. How many more 🦕
than 🦕 did you tally?

____ ◯ ____ = ____

Picture Graphs

Name _____

Make a picture graph. Draw and color one picture for each shape.

Favorite Key Chains	
	🚗 🚗
	🏀
	🐠

Use the picture graph above.

1. Which key chain was the favorite of the fewest children? Circle it.

2. Which key chain was the favorite of the most children? Circle it.

3. How many more children like than ?

____ ◯ ____ = ____   ____ more

4. How many more children like than ?

____ ◯ ____ = ____   ____ more

5. How many fewer children like than ?

____ ◯ ____ = ____   ____ fewer

Use with Lesson 4, text pages 163–164.

Pictographs

A pictograph uses a symbol to show how many.

Draw 1 for each tally mark to complete the pictograph.

Mia's Toy Collection

Toy	Tally
	|||
	|||| |
	||||

Mia's Toy Collection

Key: Each stands for 1 toy.

Use the pictograph above.

1. Which animal does Mia have the most of? Circle it.

2. Which animal does Mia have the fewest of? Circle it.

3. How many more than does Mia have?

____ ◯ ____ = _____ _____ more

4. How many toys does Mia have altogether?

____ ◯ ____ ◯ ____ = _____ _____ toys

Bar Graphs

Name _____

A bar graph uses bars to show how many.
Complete the bar graph from the tally chart.
Color 1 ☐ for each shape.

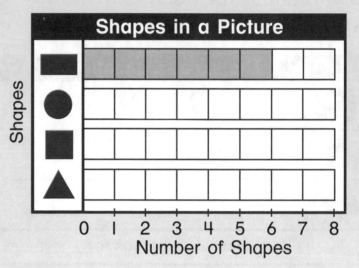

Use the bar graph above.

1. How many fewer ▲ are there than ▬?

_____ ◯ _____ = _____

2. How many more ▲ are there than ●?

_____ ◯ _____ = _____

3. How many ▬ and ■ are there in all?

_____ ◯ _____ = _____

4. Which shape is there the most of? Circle it.

5. Which shape is there the fewest of? Circle it.

6. How many ▲ and ■ are there in all?

_____ ◯ _____ = _____

Use with Lesson 6, text pages 167–168.

Surveys

Name _____

Survey people to collect information, or data, about what they like or think.

Ask 12 friends if they want to go to the river, the ocean, or the lake on their next vacation.

1. Complete the tally chart. Make a tally mark for each answer.

Favorite Vacation Place	
Place	Tally
River	
Ocean	
Lake	

2. Use your tally chart to make a bar graph.
   Color 1 ☐ for each tally.

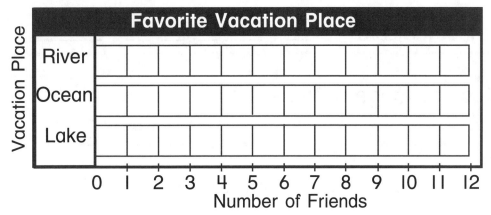

Favorite Vacation Place

Vacation Place: River, Ocean, Lake

0 1 2 3 4 5 6 7 8 9 10 11 12
Number of Friends

Use the bar graph above.

3. Which place do your friends like best? _____

4. Which place do your friends like least? _____

5. How many like the lake or the river best?    ___ ◯ ___ = ___

6. How many like the lake or the ocean best?   ___ ◯ ___ = ___

Range; Mode

Name _____

Order these numbers: 6, 1, 9, 9, 4

①, 4, 6, 9, ⑨ | 1, 4, 6, ⑨, ⑨

↑ least   ↑ greatest

The range is the greatest number minus the least.

$9 - 1 = 8$ ← range

The range is 8.

The mode is the number that you see most often in a set of data.

The mode is 9.

Use the data below to answer questions 1 through 3.

5, 6, 9, 6, 11

1. Order the numbers. ____, _____, _____, _____, _____

2. What is the range of the set of data? ____ − ____ = ____

3. What is the mode of the set of data? _____

Use the data below to answer questions 4 through 6.

6, 9, 8, 12, 8

4. Order the numbers. _____, _____, _____, _____, _____

5. What is the range of the set of data? ____ − ____ = ____

6. What is the mode of the set of data? _____

Use after Lessons 8 and 9, text pages 173–176.

Median

The median is the middle number in an ordered set of numbers.

12, 9, 7, 10, 11

To find the median, order the numbers.

7, 9, (10,) 11, 12

The median is 10.

Order the numbers. Circle the median.

1.

George's Stickers	
	7
	12
	8
	3
	3

3 ___, ___, ___, ___, ___

2.

Sandy's Beads	
	3
	6
	11
	7
	2

___, ___, ___, ___, ___

3.

Kate's Ball Collection	
	10
	4
	3
	8
	5

___, ___, ___, ___, ___

4.

Mr. Hoody's Tools	
	2
	4
	3
	8
	5

___, ___, ___, ___, ___

Problem-Solving Strategy: Use a Graph

Name _____

Read ▶ If Gabe buys two more 🐝, how many 🐝 will he have?

Gabe's Wind-up Toys	
🐝	🙂 🙂 🙂 🙂
🤖	🙂 🙂
👹	🙂 🙂 🙂 🙂 🙂 🙂

Key: Each 🙂 stands for 1 toy.

Plan ▶ Use the graph. Count how many 🐝. Write a number sentence.

Write ▶ Gabe has 4 🐝. Add 2 more.

$$4 + 2 = 6$$

Gabe will have 6 🐝.

Check ▶ Draw a picture to show how many 🐝.

Use the pictograph above to solve each problem.

1. How many fewer 🤖 than 🐝 does Gabe have?   Gabe has ____ fewer 🤖 than 🐝.

---

2. If Gabe buys 3 more 🤖, how many 🤖 will he have?   Gabe will have ____ 🤖.

---

3. How many more 👹 than 🐝 does Gabe have?   Gabe has ____ more 👹 than 🐝.

Use with Lesson 10, text pages 181–182.

Problem-Solving Applications: Mixed Strategies

Name _____

Read ▸ **Plan** ▸ **Write** ▸ **Check**

Use a strategy you have learned.

Books Read During Vacation	
Jonah	✔ ✔ ✔ ✔
Ty	✔ ✔ ✔
Sammy	✔ ✔ ✔ ✔ ✔ ✔
Key: Each ✔ stands for 1 book.	

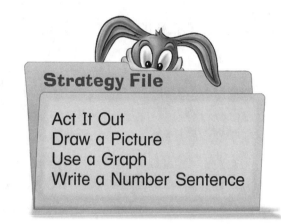

Strategy File

Act It Out
Draw a Picture
Use a Graph
Write a Number Sentence

Use the graph above for problems 1–3.

1. Who read twice as many books as Ty?
   Circle your answer.   Jonah   Sammy

2. How many books in all do Ty and Sammy read?

   _____ books in all.

3. How many fewer books does Jonah read than Sammy?

   _____ fewer books.

4. Emily has 3 🦀 and 4 🐙.
   She also has 3 🦆.
   How many stuffed animals does Emily have in all?

   Emily has _____ stuffed animals in all.

5. Tim has 8 🚗.
   Deb has 3 fewer 🚗 than Tim.
   How many 🚗 does Deb have?

   Deb has _____ 🚗.

Tens and Ones

Name _____

Make groups of 10 to find how many tens and ones.

2 groups of 10 and 4 more.

2 tens 4 ones

Circle groups of 10.
Write how many tens and ones.

1.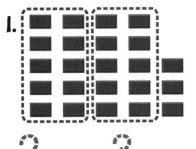

__2__ tens __3__ ones

2.

____ tens ____ ones

3.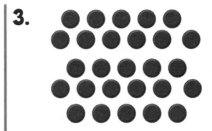

____ tens ____ ones

4.

____ ten ____ ones

5.

____ ten ____ ones

6.

____ tens ____ ones

7.

____ tens ____ one

8.

____ tens ____ ones

9.

____ ten ____ ones

Use with Lesson 1, text pages 195–196.

Tens Through One Hundred

Name _____

You can use models to count by tens.

1 ten	2 tens	3 tens	4 tens	5 tens
10	20	30	40	50
ten	twenty	thirty	forty	fifty

Write how many tens.
Write the number and the number word.

1.  __3__ tens = 30

thirty

2. 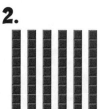 ___ tens = ___

sixty

3.  ___ tens = ___

fifty

4. 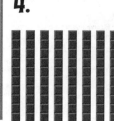 ___ tens = ___

eighty

Write the number.

5. 2 tens = ___

6. 7 tens = ___

7. 3 tens = ___

8. 9 tens = ___

9. 1 ten = ___

10. 6 tens = ___

11. 4 tens = ___

12. 10 tens = ___

13. 9 tens = ___

14. 8 tens = ___

15. 5 tens = ___

16. 1 ten = ___

Use with Lesson 2, text pages 197–198.

Numbers 11 Through 19

Thirteen is 1 group of ten and 3 ones.

tens	ones

eleven twelve thirteen fourteen fifteen
sixteen seventeen eighteen nineteen

1 ten 3 ones

13

thirteen

Write the number and the number word.

1.    _17_

seventeen

2.    _____

_____

Write the number.

3. 1 ten 4 ones _____

4. 1 ten 8 ones _____

5. 1 ten 9 ones _____

6. 1 ten 1 one _____

7. 1 ten 6 ones _____

8. 1 ten 2 ones _____

9. 1 ten 3 ones _____

10. 1 ten 0 ones _____

11. 1 ten 5 ones _____

12. 1 ten 7 ones _____

Use with Lesson 3, text pages 199–200.

Numbers
20 Through 39

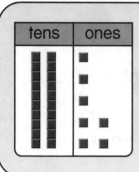

2 tens 7 ones
27
twenty-seven

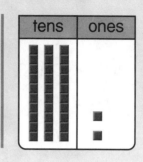

3 tens 2 ones
32
thirty-two

Write how many.

1.

__3__ tens __0__ ones

__30__ thirty

2.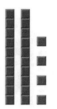

___ tens ___ ones

___ twenty-four

3.

___ tens ___ ones

___ thirty-eight

4.

___ tens ___ ones

___ twenty-five

5.

___ tens ___ one

___ thirty-one

6.

___ tens ___ ones

___ twenty

7.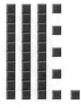

___ tens ___ ones

___ thirty-six

8.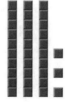

___ tens ___ ones

___ thirty-three

9.

___ tens ___ ones

___ twenty-nine

Numbers
40 Through 59

Name _____

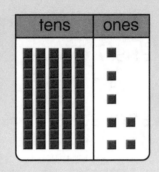

tens	ones			tens	ones		

4 tens 2 ones
42
forty-two

5 tens 7 ones
57
fifty-seven

Write how many.

1.

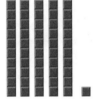

$\underline{5}$ tens $\underline{1}$ one

$\underline{51}$ fifty-one

2.

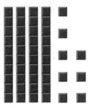

___ tens ___ ones

___ forty-eight

3.

___ tens ___ ones

___ forty

4.

___ tens ___ ones

___ fifty-three

5.

___ tens ___ ones

___ forty-four

6.

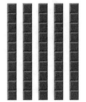

___ tens ___ ones

___ fifty

7.

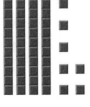

___ tens ___ ones

___ forty-seven

8.

___ tens ___ ones

___ forty-five

9.

___ tens ___ ones

___ fifty-nine

Use with Lesson 5, text pages 203–204.

Numbers
60 Through 89

Name _____

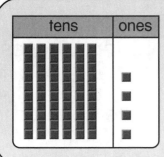 | 6 tens 4 ones
64
sixty-four

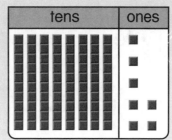 | 8 tens 7 ones
87
eighty-seven

Write how many.

1.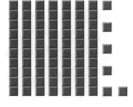

__7__ tens __6__ ones

__76__ seventy-six

2.

____ tens ____ ones

____ eighty-eight

3.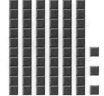

____ tens ____ ones

____ sixty-three

4.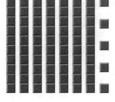

____ tens ____ ones

____ seventy-five

5.

____ tens ____ one

____ sixty-one

6.

____ tens ____ ones

____ eighty

7.

____ tens ____ ones

____ seventy-eight

8.

____ tens ____ ones

____ eighty-nine

9.

____ tens ____ ones

____ sixty-two

Use with Lesson 6, text pages 205–206.

Numbers
90 Through 100

Name _____

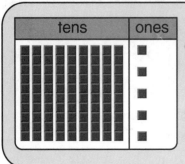

tens	ones

9 tens 5 ones
95
ninety-five

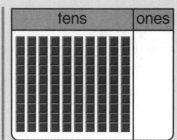

tens	ones

10 tens 0 ones
100
one hundred

Write how many.

1.
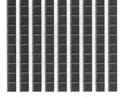

__9__ tens __0__ ones

__90__ ninety

2.
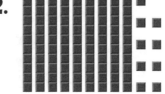

___ tens ___ ones

___ ninety-nine

3.

___ tens ___ ones

___ ninety-three

4.
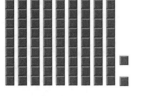

___ tens ___ ones

___ ninety-two

5.

___ tens ___ ones

___ ninety-six

6.
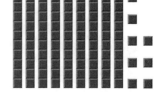

___ tens ___ ones

___ ninety-eight

7.
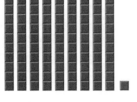

___ tens ___ one

___ ninety-one

8.
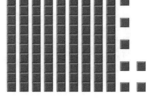

___ tens ___ ones

___ ninety-seven

9.

___ tens ___ ones

___ ninety-four

Use with Lesson 7, text pages 207–208.

Estimate Quantities

Name _____

Use the 10  to estimate, or make
a good guess, about how many.

10 shells ←

about 20

about 30

About how many of each are there?
Circle your estimate.

1.

10 sand dollars

about 20

about 40

2.

10 shells

about 20

about 40

3.

10 shells

about 20

about 30

4.

10 shells

about 30

about 40

5.

10 sand dollars

about 20

about 30

6.

10 shells

about 20

about 40

Place Value of Digits; Expanded Form

Name _____

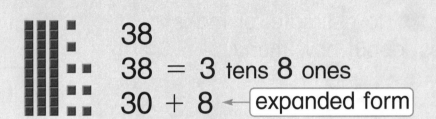

38

38 = 3 tens 8 ones

30 + 8 ← expanded form

Circle the value of the underlined digit.

1. 67
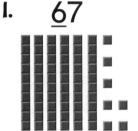

6

(60)

2. 53
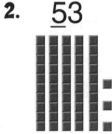

5

50

3. 21

1

10

4. 98

8   80

5. 76

7   70

6. 19

9   90

7. 35

3   30

8. 44

4   40

9. 82

2   20

Write the number for each expanded form.

10.

30 + 4 = _____

11.

90 + 5 = _____

12.

40 + 7 = _____

13.

70 + 8 = _____

14.

80 + 6 = _____

15.

60 + 9 = _____

One Less, One More

Name _____

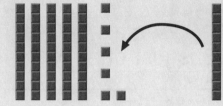

56 is one less than 57. | 57 | 58 is one more than 57.

Count on I.
Write the number that is I more.

1. 63, _64_ | **2.** 90, ___ | **3.** 29, ___

4. 69, ___ | **5.** 44, ___ | **6.** 72, ___

Count back I.
Write the number that is I less.

7. ___, 80 | **8.** ___, 39 | **9.** ___, 86

10. ___, 90 | **11.** ___, 20 | **12.** ___, 57

Count on or back. Write the number that is
I less and the number that is I more.

13. ___, 96, ___ | **14.** ___, 40, ___ | **15.** ___, 79, ___

16. ___, 71, ___ | **17.** ___, 46, ___ | **18.** ___, 53, ___

Identify Before, Between, After

Name _____

Write the number that comes between.

1. 76 [77] 78

2. 34 [ ] 36

3. 19 [ ] 21

4. 55 [ ] 57

5. 41 [ ] 43

6. 28 [ ] 30

Write the numbers that come just before and just after.

7. [33] 34 [35]

8. [ ] 69 [ ]

9. [ ] 81 [ ]

10. [ ] 52 [ ]

11. [ ] 98 [ ]

12. [ ] 29 [ ]

13. [ ] 18 [ ]

14. [ ] 50 [ ]

15. [ ] 63 [ ]

Use with Lesson 12, text pages 219–220.

Compare Numbers

Name _____

Compare 55 and 29.	Compare 63 and 67.	Compare 18 and 18.
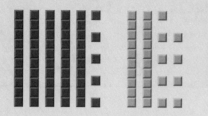	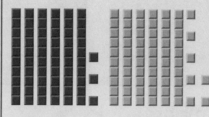	
55 has more tens.	Both have 6 tens. 63 has fewer ones.	Both have 1 ten. Both have 8 ones.
55 is greater than 29.	63 is less than 67.	They are equal.
55 > 29	63 < 67	18 = 18

Compare. Write <, =, or >.

1. 21 31   **2.** 47 ◯ 41   **3.** 22 ◯ 19

4. 56 ◯ 96   **5.** 74 ◯ 47   **6.** 44 ◯ 44

7. 81 ◯ 81   **8.** 29 ◯ 33   **9.** 65 ◯ 66

10. 63 ◯ 36   **11.** 58 ◯ 95   **12.** 98 ◯ 98

Write the numbers to show which is greater or less.

13. 37   73   **14.** 85   83   **15.** 51   49

_____ > _____ | _____ < _____ | _____ > _____

16. 62   26   **17.** 39   37   **18.** 44   54

_____ < _____ | _____ > _____ | _____ < _____

Use with Lesson 13, text pages 221–222.

Order Numbers

A number line can help you put numbers in order.

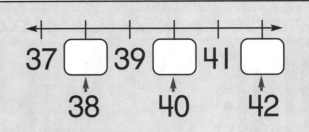

37 ☐ 39 ☐ 41 ☐
38 40 42

Write the missing numbers.

1.
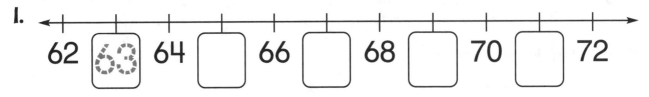
62 **63** 64 ☐ 66 ☐ 68 ☐ 70 ☐ 72

2.
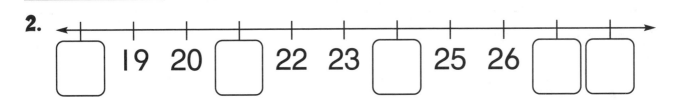
☐ 19 20 ☐ 22 23 ☐ 25 26 ☐ ☐

3.
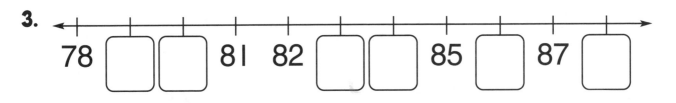
78 ☐ ☐ 81 82 ☐ ☐ 85 ☐ 87 ☐

4.
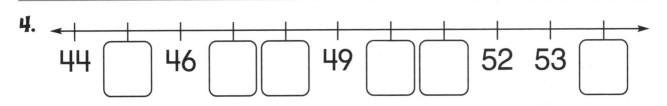
44 ☐ 46 ☐ ☐ 49 ☐ ☐ 52 53 ☐

5.
68 ☐ ☐ 71 72 73 ☐ ☐ 76 77 78

6.
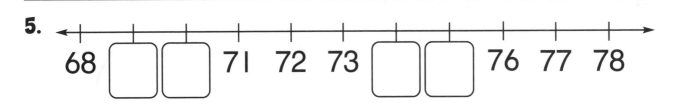
33 ☐ 35 36 37 ☐ ☐ ☐ 41 42 43

Use with Lesson 14, text pages 223–224.

Hundred-Chart Patterns; 10 Less, 10 More

1. Complete the hundred chart.

1		3		5		7		9	
	12		14		16		18		20
21		23		25		27		29	
	32		34		36		38		40
41		43		45		47		49	
	52		54		56		58		60
61		63		65		67		69	
	72		74		76		78		80
81		83		85		87		89	
	92		94		96		98		100

Write the number that is 10 more or 10 less.

2. 66, 76

3. 19, _____

4. 50, _____

5. 8, _____

6. 71, _____

7. 34, _____

8. _____, 14

9. _____, 100

10. _____, 53

11. 71, _____

12. 35, _____

13. _____, 42

Even and Odd

Name _____

Make pairs to decide even or odd.

8 is an even number.
None are left over.

7 is an odd number.
One is left over.

Write the number in all. Circle pairs.
Is the number even or odd?

1.

_6_ is _even_.

2.

_____ is _____.

3.

_____ is _____.

4.

_____ is _____.

5.

_____ is _____.

6.

_____ is _____.

7.

_____ is _____.

8.

_____ is _____.

Use with Lesson 18, text pages 233–234.

Count by 5s

1. Count by 5s to complete
the hundred chart.

1	2	3	4		6	7	8	9	
11	12	13	14	15	16	17	18	19	20
21	22	23	24		26	27	28	29	30
31	32	33	34	35	36	37	38	39	
41	42	43	44	45	46	47	48	49	50
51	52	53	54		56	57	58	59	60
61	62	63	64	65	66	67	68	69	
71	72	73	74		76	77	78	79	80
81	82	83	84	85	86	87	88	89	90
91	92	93	94		96	97	98	99	

2. Color the count–by–5 numbers on the chart.

Count by 5s. Write the missing numbers.

3. 60, 65, _70_, ____, 80, ____, ____, 95, ____

4. 25, ____, ____, 40, ____, ____, 55, ____, ____

5. ____, 10, ____, ____, 25, ____, 35, ____, ____

Count by 2s

1. Count by 2s to complete the hundred chart.

1		3	4	5		7	8	9	
11	12	13		15	16	17		19	20
21		23	24	25		27	28	29	
31	32	33		35	36	37		39	40
41		43		45		47	48	49	
51	52	53	54	55	56	57		59	60
61		63		65	66	67		69	
71	72	73	74	75		77	78	79	80
81		83	84	85	86	87	88	89	90
91	92	93	94	95		97		99	

2. Color the count–by–2 numbers on the chart.

Count by 2s. Write the missing numbers.

3. 70, 72, 74, ____, ____, ____, ____, 84, ____

4. 55, ____, ____, 61, ____, ____, 67, ____, ____

5. 48, 46, ____, ____, 40, ____, ____, 34, ____

Use with Lesson 20, text pages 237–238.

Problem-Solving Strategy: Logical Reasoning

Name _____

Read ▶ Ella spins and gets a number.
It is greater than 30.
It is less than 40.
It has 3 ones.
What number does Ella get?

28	33
41	37

Plan ▶ Use clues to make a list
to help solve the problem.

Write ▶ Which numbers on the
spinner are greater than 30? _33_, _37_, _41_

Which of those numbers
are less than 40? _33_, _37_

Which of those numbers
has 3 ones? _33_

Check ▶ Does your answer match the clues?

---

1. Mark spins and gets a number.
The number is greater than 10.
It is less than 20.
It has 1 one.
What number does Mark get?

Mark gets _____.

---

2. Jules spins and gets a number.
The number is greater than 70.
It is less than 90.
It has no ones in the ones place.
What number does Jules get?

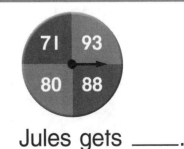

Jules gets _____.

Problem-Solving Applications: Mixed Strategies

Name _____

Read ⟩ **Plan** ⟩ **Write** ⟩ **Check**

Use a strategy you have learned.

1. Marci writes a number
between 30 and 40.
It has 9 ones.
What number does Marci write?

Marci writes _____.

---

2. Paula counts 9 in the store.
She counts a dozen .
How many more than
does Paula count?

Paula counts _____ more .

---

3. Cleon writes three numbers between 6 and 20.
They are 1-digit numbers.
What numbers does Cleon write?

_____, _____, _____

---

4. Ruth has 5 tens 4 ones.
Paul has 10 more than Ruth.
Di has 1 less than Paul.
What numbers do they have?

Ruth _____, Paul _____, Di _____

Sums Through 14

Name _____

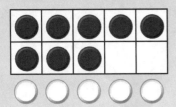 8 + 5 = ?

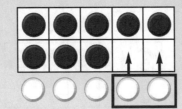 Make 10.

8 + 2 = 10
10 + 3 = 13
So 8 + 5 = 13.

Add.

1.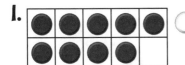

9 + 5 = _14_

2.

8 + 6 = ___

3.

7 + 7 = ___

4.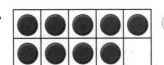

9 + 4 = ___

5.   4
      + 9
      1 3

6.   5
      + 8

7.   7
      + 7

8.   9
      + 4

9.   8
      + 5

10. 6 + 7 = ___

11. 7 + 6 = ___

12. 5 + 9 = ___

13. 8 + 6 = ___

14. 9 + 5 = ___

15. 5 + 8 = ___

Use with Lesson 1, text pages 257–258.

Sums Through 16

Name _____

$6 + 9 = ?$

Model the addends.

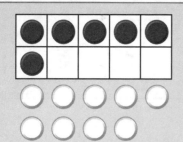

Fill the ten-frame to make 10.

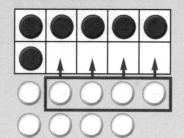

$6 + 4 = 10$

$10 + 5 = 15$

So $6 + 9 = 15$.

Make 10. Then add.

1.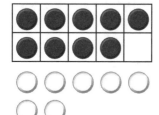

$$\begin{array}{r} 9 \\ + 7 \\ \hline 16 \end{array}$$

2.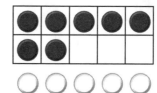

$$\begin{array}{r} 7 \\ + 9 \\ \hline \end{array}$$

3.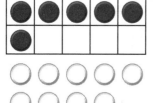

$6 + 9 =$ ___

4.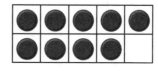

$9 + 6 =$ ___

5.
$$\begin{array}{r} 8 \\ + 8 \\ \hline 16 \end{array}$$

6.
$$\begin{array}{r} 7 \\ + 8 \\ \hline \end{array}$$

7.
$$\begin{array}{r} 8 \\ + 7 \\ \hline \end{array}$$

8.
$$\begin{array}{r} 8 \\ + 5 \\ \hline \end{array}$$

9.
$$\begin{array}{r} 7 \\ + 6 \\ \hline \end{array}$$

10.

$9 + 7 =$ ___

11.

$8 + 7 =$ ___

12.

$6 + 7 =$ ___

Use with Lesson 2, text pages 259–260.

Sums Through 18

8 + 9 = ?
8 + 8 = 16
8 + 9 is 1 more.
So 8 + 9 = 17.

Make 10 to add.
9 + 9 = ?
9 + 1 = 10
10 + 8 = 18
So 9 + 9 = 18.

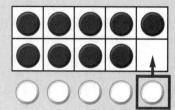

Write the second addend. Then add.

1.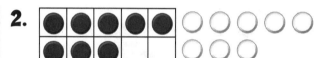

$9 + \underline{6} = \underline{15}$

2.

$8 + \underline{} = \underline{}$

3.

$9 + \underline{} = \underline{}$

4.

$9 + \underline{} = \underline{}$

Find the sum.

5.
$\begin{array}{r} 8 \\ + 9 \\ \hline 17 \end{array}$

6.
$\begin{array}{r} 7 \\ + 9 \\ \hline \end{array}$

7.
$\begin{array}{r} 8 \\ + 8 \\ \hline \end{array}$

8.
$\begin{array}{r} 9 \\ + 9 \\ \hline \end{array}$

9.
$\begin{array}{r} 6 \\ + 9 \\ \hline \end{array}$

10.
$\begin{array}{r} 9 \\ + 5 \\ \hline \end{array}$

11.
$9 + 7 = \underline{}$

12.
$5 + 9 = \underline{}$

13.
$8 + 7 = \underline{}$

14.
$7 + 7 = \underline{}$

15.
$6 + 8 = \underline{}$

16.
$9 + 9 = \underline{}$

Use with Lesson 3, text pages 261–262.

Subtract from 13 and 14

Name _____

$14 - 6 = ?$

Subtract.	Add to check.

$$\begin{array}{r} 14 \\ -\ 6 \\ \hline 8 \end{array} \qquad \begin{array}{r} 8 \\ +\ 6 \\ \hline 14 \end{array}$$

$14 - 6 = 8$

Subtract. Add to check.

1.

$13 \quad - \quad 4 \quad = \quad 9$

___ + ___ = ___

2.

$14 \quad - \quad 9 \quad = \quad$ ___

___ + ___ = ___

3.

$14 \quad - \quad 5 \quad = \quad$ ___

___ + ___ = ___

4.

$13 \quad - \quad 8 \quad = \quad$ ___

___ + ___ = ___

5.
$$\begin{array}{r} 13 \\ -\ 9 \\ \hline 4 \end{array} \qquad \begin{array}{r} 4 \\ +\ 9 \\ \hline 13 \end{array}$$

6.
$$\begin{array}{r} 14 \\ -\ 7 \\ \hline \end{array} \quad + \begin{array}{r} \square \\ \square \\ \hline \end{array}$$

7.
$$\begin{array}{r} 14 \\ -\ 8 \\ \hline \end{array} \quad + \begin{array}{r} \square \\ \square \\ \hline \end{array}$$

8. $13 \quad - \quad 5 \quad = \quad$ ___

___ + ___ = ___

9. $13 \quad - \quad 7 \quad = \quad$ ___

___ + ___ = ___

Use with Lesson 5, text pages 267–268.

Subtract from 16 or Less

Name _____

$$16 - 7 = ?$$
$$16 - 7 = 9$$

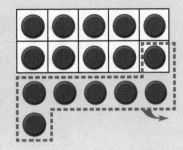

Subtract. Circle the part taken away.

1. $\begin{array}{r} 15 \\ -9 \\ \hline 6 \end{array}$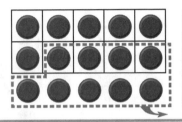

2. $\begin{array}{r} 14 \\ -9 \\ \hline \end{array}$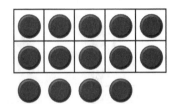

3. $\begin{array}{r} 15 \\ -7 \\ \hline \end{array}$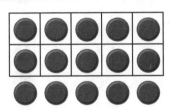

4. $\begin{array}{r} 16 \\ -8 \\ \hline \end{array}$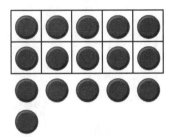

5. $\begin{array}{r} 16 \\ -9 \\ \hline \end{array}$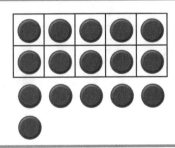

6. $\begin{array}{r} 15 \\ -6 \\ \hline \end{array}$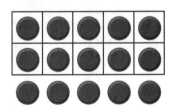

Find the difference. Use ⊞ and ⬤ to help.

7. $\begin{array}{r} 14 \\ -7 \\ \hline \end{array}$ **8.** $\begin{array}{r} 14 \\ -6 \\ \hline \end{array}$ **9.** $\begin{array}{r} 15 \\ -8 \\ \hline \end{array}$ **10.** $\begin{array}{r} 15 \\ -7 \\ \hline \end{array}$ **11.** $\begin{array}{r} 16 \\ -9 \\ \hline \end{array}$

12. $16 - 7 = $ ___   **13.** $16 - 9 = $ ___   **14.** $16 - 8 = $ ___

Subtract from 18 or Less

Name _____

$18 - 9 = ?$ 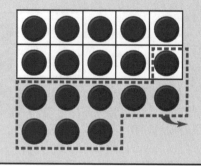 $18 - 9 = 9$

Subtract.

1. $\begin{array}{r} 15 \\ -\ 6 \\ \hline 9 \end{array}$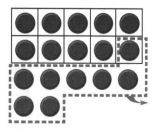

2. $\begin{array}{r} 17 \\ -\ 9 \\ \hline \end{array}$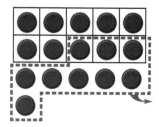

3. $\begin{array}{r} 17 \\ -\ 8 \\ \hline \end{array}$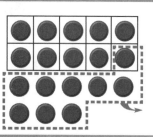

4. $\begin{array}{r} 16 \\ -\ 9 \\ \hline \end{array}$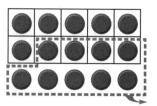

5. $\begin{array}{r} 18 \\ -\ 9 \\ \hline \end{array}$

6. $\begin{array}{r} 15 \\ -\ 9 \\ \hline \end{array}$

7. $\begin{array}{r} 16 \\ -\ 8 \\ \hline 8 \end{array}$

8. $\begin{array}{r} 17 \\ -\ 9 \\ \hline \end{array}$

9. $\begin{array}{r} 16 \\ -\ 7 \\ \hline \end{array}$

10. $\begin{array}{r} 15 \\ -\ 8 \\ \hline \end{array}$

11. $17 - 8 = $ _____

12. $16 - 9 = $ _____

13. $15 - 7 = $ _____

Use with Lesson 7, text pages 271–272.

More Fact Families

7	4	11	
+	−	=	

A fact family shows all the related facts.

7	+	4	=	11
4	+	7	=	11
11	−	4	=	7
11	−	7	=	4

Write each fact family.

1. | 15 | 6 | 9 |

6 $\oplus$ 9 = <u>15</u>

<u>9</u> $\oplus$ <u>6</u> = ___

___ $\ominus$ ___ = ___

___ $\ominus$ ___ = ___

2. | 16 | 7 | 9 |

7 ◯ 9 = ___

___ ◯ ___ = ___

___ ◯ ___ = ___

___ ◯ ___ = ___

3. | 9 | 18 |

___ ◯ ___ = ___

___ ◯ ___ = ___

4. | 8 | 16 |

___ ◯ ___ = ___

___ ◯ ___ = ___

5.

8	☐	☐	☐

$\oplus$ 6 ◯ ◯ ◯

<u>14</u>

6.

8	☐	☐	☐

◯ 9 ◯ ◯ ◯

Three Addends

Name _____

You can change the order to add.

Add down.	Add up.	Make 10.	Use doubles.
2	5	7	3
7 → 9	3 5	1 → 10	3 → 6
+ 5 + 5	+ 4 → + 7	+ 3 + 1	+ 2 + 2
14	12	11	8

Add. Circle the numbers you add first.

1.
6
4
+ 2

+ 10
  2
  12

2.
3
6
+ 4

+ ☐
  ☐

3.
2
7
+ 5

+ ☐
  ☐

4.
7
3
+ 4

+ ☐
  ☐

5.
3
3
+ 6

+ ☐
  ☐

6.
1
8
+ 2

+ ☐
  ☐

7.
6
3
+ 2

+ ☐
  ☐

8.
9
3
+ 0

+ ☐
  ☐

9.
5
4
+ 4

+ ☐
  ☐

10. $7 + 0 + 8 = \ ?$

___ + ___ = ___

11. $4 + 5 + 1 = \ ?$

___ + ___ = ___

Use with Lesson 9, text pages 277–278.

Extending Facts to 20

$9 + 10 = ?$

Use a doubles fact.

$9 + 9 = 18$

10 is one more than 9.

So $9 + 10 = 19.$

$20 - 10 = ?$

Take away 10.

$20 - 10 = 10$

Add or subtract.

1.
$9 + 9 = \underline{18}$

2.
$8 + 7 = \underline{}$

3.
$9 + 8 = \underline{}$

4.
$10 + 9 = \underline{}$

5.
$19 - 9 = \underline{}$

6.
$8 + 9 = \underline{}$

7.
$20 - 10 = \underline{}$

8.
$15 - 9 = \underline{}$

9.
$7 + 9 = \underline{}$

10.
$17 - 9 = \underline{}$

11.
$16 - 7 = \underline{}$

12.
$8 + 8 = \underline{}$

13.
$\begin{array}{r} 18 \\ -\ 9 \\ \hline 9 \end{array}$

14.
$\begin{array}{r} 17 \\ -\ 8 \\ \hline \end{array}$

15.
$\begin{array}{r} 9 \\ +\ 6 \\ \hline \end{array}$

16.
$\begin{array}{r} 8 \\ +\ 7 \\ \hline \end{array}$

17.
$\begin{array}{r} 20 \\ -10 \\ \hline \end{array}$

18.
$\begin{array}{r} 7 \\ +\ 7 \\ \hline \end{array}$

19.
$\begin{array}{r} 16 \\ -\ 7 \\ \hline \end{array}$

20.
$\begin{array}{r} 10 \\ +10 \\ \hline \end{array}$

21.
$\begin{array}{r} 15 \\ -\ 8 \\ \hline \end{array}$

22.
$\begin{array}{r} 10 \\ +\ 9 \\ \hline \end{array}$

Missing Part of a Number Sentence

$8 + ? = 12$	**Count up.**	**Use a subtraction fact.**
	$8 + ? = 12$	$8 + ? = 12$
	Count up from 8: 9, 10, 11, 12	$12 - 8 = 4$
	$8 + 4 = 12$	So $8 + 4 = 12$.

What number will make each number sentence true?
Use to help.

1. $7 + \boxed{9} = 16$

2. $8 + \boxed{} = 13$

3. $\boxed{} + 4 = 11$

4. $17 - \boxed{} = 9$

5. $\boxed{} + 10 = 20$

6. $14 - \boxed{} = 5$

7. $6 + \boxed{} = 13$

8. $\boxed{} + 10 = 19$

9. $\boxed{} + 7 = 14$

10. $17 - \boxed{} = 8$

11. $9 + \boxed{} = 12$

12. $\boxed{} - 9 = 9$

13. $11 - \boxed{} = 3$

14. $9 + \boxed{} = 16$

Use with Lesson 11, text pages 281–282.

Open and Closed Figures; Sides and Corners

Name _____

A closed flat figure is a plane figure.

vertex (corner)

closed figure ←side   open figure

An open figure is not a plane figure.

Draw to make each a closed figure.

1.    2.    3. 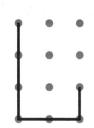   4.

Trace each figure.
Draw a ● at each vertex.
Write how many sides and corners.

5.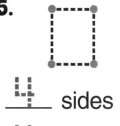

___4___ sides

___4___ corners

6.

_____ sides

_____ corners

7.

_____ sides

_____ corners

8.

_____ sides

_____ corners

9.

_____ sides

_____ corners

10.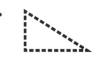

_____ sides

_____ corners

11.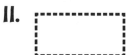

_____ sides

_____ corners

12.

_____ sides

_____ corners

Sorting Plane Figures

Name _____

4 square corners	0 square corners	4 corners
rectangle square	triangle circle	trapezoid

Sort the figures.

Circle the figures that follow each rule.

	Rule	Figures
1.	0 corners	
2.	3 corners and 3 sides	
3.	4 square corners and 4 sides	
4.	5 corners and 5 sides	
5.	1 square corner and 3 sides	
6.	4 corners and 4 sides	

Use with Lesson 3, text pages 301–302.

Ways to Make Figures

Name _____

You can make a plane figure or take apart
a plane figure using different shapes.

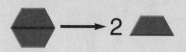

Use pattern blocks to make a new figure.
How many of each pattern block did you use?

1. Use ▲ to make a .

2. Use ◆ to make a .

<u>3</u> ▲ make 1 .

_____ ◆ make 1 .

3. Use ▲ to make a .

4. Use ▲ to make a ◆.

_____ ▲ make 1 .

_____ ▲ make 1 .

Draw lines to show how to make different shapes.
Use pattern blocks to help.

5. 2

6. 3 ▲

7. 6 ▲

Solid Figures;
Attributes of Solid Figures

Name _____

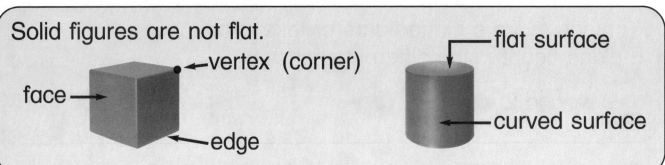

Solid figures are not flat.

face → | vertex (corner)

edge

flat surface

curved surface

Color the figures that have the same shape.

1.  rectangular prism |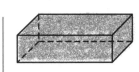

2.   cylinder |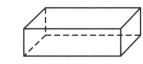

3. pyramid |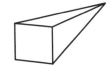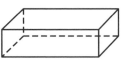

What does the arrow point to?
Circle the correct math word.

4.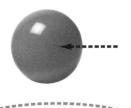

(curved surface)

vertex

5.

edge

face

6.

curved surface

flat surface

Use after Lessons 5 and 6, text pages 307–310.

Plane Figures on Solid Figures

Name _____

The flat surfaces of solid figures are shaped like plane figures.

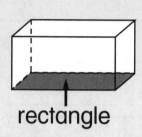 rectangle

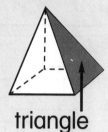 triangle

 circle

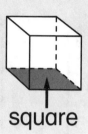 square

Circle any solid figure with a flat surface that matches the plane figure at the beginning of each row.

1. |

2. |

3. |

Write **square**, **triangle**, or **circle**.

4. The face of a cube is a _____square_____.

5. Four faces of a pyramid are _____.

6. Each flat surface of a cylinder is a _____.

7. The flat surface of a cone is a _____.

Graphing Attributes

Name _____

1. Make a bar graph for each.
Color 1 box for each side on the plane figures.

Sides of Plane Figures

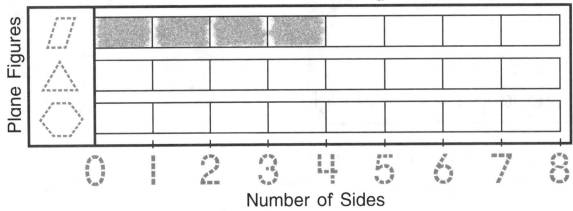

Number of Sides

2. Color 1 box for each corner on the solid figures.

Corners of Solid Figures

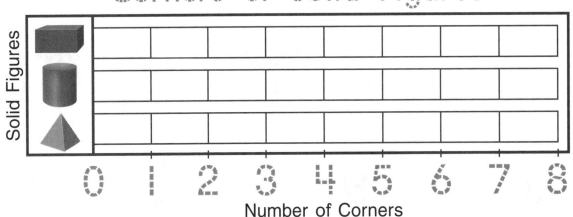

Number of Corners

3. Color 1 box for each face on the solid figures.

Faces on Solid Figures

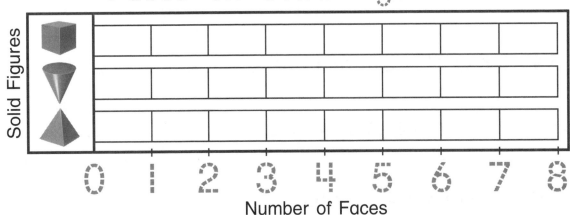

Number of Faces

Use with Lesson 8, text pages 313–314.

Roll, Slide, and Stack

Name _____

Solid figures can move in different ways.

A sphere has a curved surface.	A rectangular prism has a flat surface.	A cylinder has flat surfaces on the top and bottom.

A sphere can roll.	A rectangular prism can slide.	A cylinder can stack.

Circle solid figures to show
if they roll, slide, or stack.

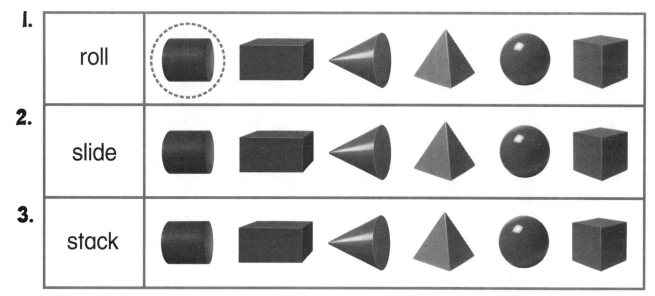

1.	roll						
2.	slide						
3.	stack						

4. Color each solid figure that both rolls and slides.

5. Color each solid figure that both stacks and rolls.

Slides and Flips

Name _____

Plane figures can move in different ways.

A slide moves a figure along a line.	A flip turns a figure over.

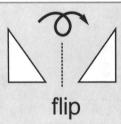

slide   flip

Model each slide or flip.
Trace the shape to show how it was moved.

1. Flip the 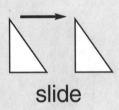 .

2. Slide the 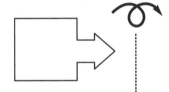 .

3. Slide the 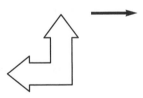 .

4. Flip the  .

Look for a slide pattern or a flip pattern.
Draw what is most likely to come next.

5.   _____

6.  _____

Use with Lesson 10, text pages 319–320.

Slides and Turns

Name _____

A figure can slide to the right, left, up, or down.	A figure can turn around a point.
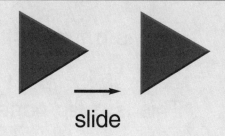 slide	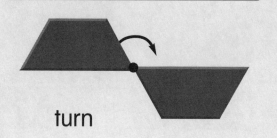 turn

Model each slide or turn.
Trace the shape to show how it was moved.

1. Slide the 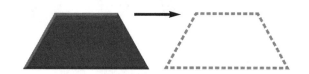.

2. Turn the .

3. Turn the .

4. Slide the .

Look for a slide pattern or a turn pattern.
Draw what is most likely to come next.

5.

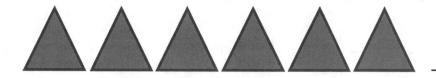

6.

Use with Lesson 11, text pages 321–322.

Pattern Rules

Name _____

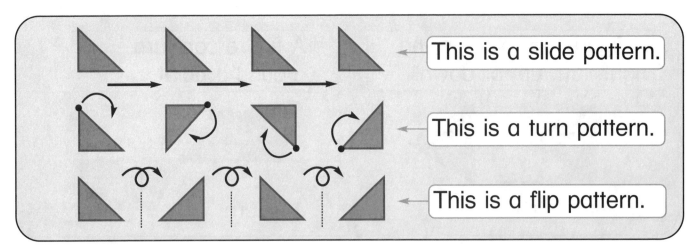

This is a slide pattern.

This is a turn pattern.

This is a flip pattern.

Write **slide**, **turn**, or **flip** to describe each pattern.
Circle what comes next in each pattern.

1.

This is a ____slide____ pattern.

2.

This is a _____ pattern.

3.

This is a _____ pattern.

4.

This is a _____ pattern.

Use with Lesson 12, text pages 323–324.

Give and Follow Directions

Name _____

Where is the ▱ ?
To find out, start at 0.

Count across.
Count up.

The ▱ is 9 across
and 7 up.

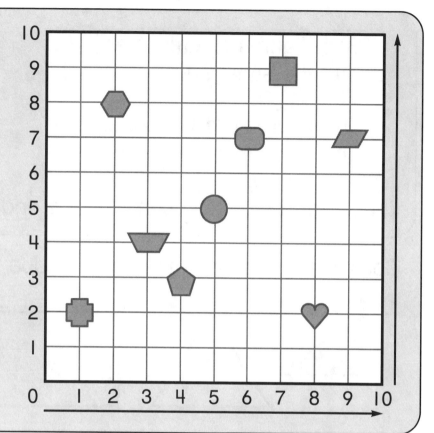

Use the grid above.
Write the numbers to tell where each figure is.

	Figure	Across	Up
1.	⬠	4	3
2.	✚		
3.	♥		
4.	⬡		

	Figure	Across	Up
5.	▽		
6.	◼		
7.	●		
8.	▬		

Look at the grid. Circle the correct answer.

9. Is the ● to the right
or left of the ◼?   right   left

10. Is the ● above or below the ?   above   below

Same Shape and Size

Name _____

> Both figures are triangles with the same shape.
>
> The figures are the same size. The sides match exactly.
>
>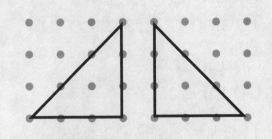
>
> These figures are the same shape and the same size.

Color the figures with the same shape and the same size.

1.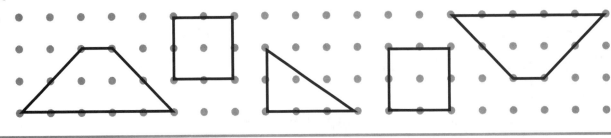

2.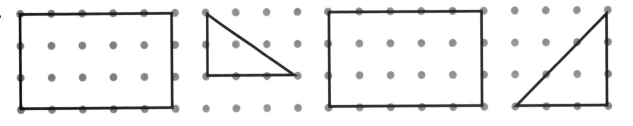

3.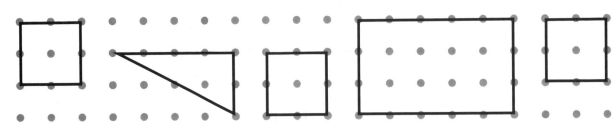

4.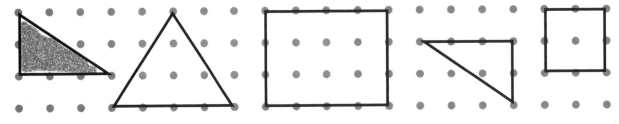

Use with Lesson 15, text pages 331–332.

Symmetry

> Shapes with symmetry have matching parts.
>
> The fold line is the line of symmetry.

Look for a line of symmetry. Circle the shape that shows matching parts.

1.

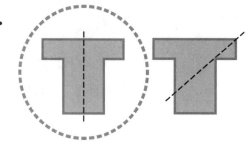

2.

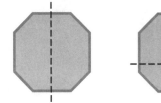

3.

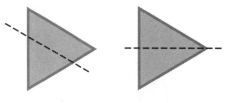

4.

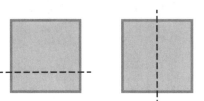

5.

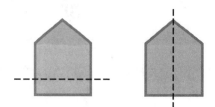

6.

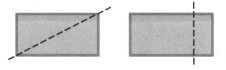

7.

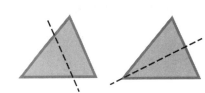

8.

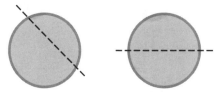

9.

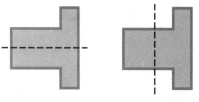

10.

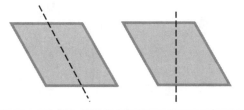

11.

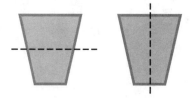

Problem-Solving Strategy: Find/Use a Pattern

Name _____

Read How can you show this pattern using numbers?

Plan Look for a pattern rule.
Think of the parts that repeat.
The pattern rule is 1 circle, then 3 rectangles.
Show the same pattern with the numbers 1 and 3.

Write

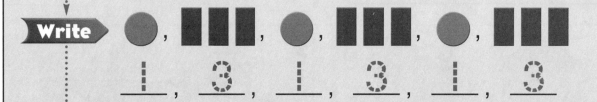

$\underline{1}$, $\underline{3}$, $\underline{1}$, $\underline{3}$, $\underline{1}$, $\underline{3}$

Check Does your number pattern follow the same rule as the shape pattern?

Find a pattern. Show the same pattern using numbers.

1.

$\underline{3}$, $\underline{2}$, _____ , _____ , _____ , _____

2.

_____ , _____ , _____ , _____ , _____ , _____

3.

_____ , _____ , _____ , _____ , _____ , _____

Use with Lesson 17, text pages 335–336.

Problem-Solving Applications: Mixed Strategies

Name _____

 Read Plan Write Check

Use a strategy you have learned.

1. Bari makes a pattern with these shapes. Show the same pattern using numbers.

_____ , _____ , _____ , _____ , _____ , _____

---

2. Bill spins and gets a number.
The number is less than 100.
It is more than 90.
It has 3 ones.
What number does Bill get?

Bill gets _____.

---

3. I can slide.
I cannot roll.
I have 4 faces.
What figure am I?
Circle your answer.

---

4. Dusty spends 8¢ on a .
He pays with a dime.
How much does Dusty have left?

Dusty has _____ left.

Nickels and Pennies

Name _____

Count on by 5s for nickels.	Count on by 1s for pennies.

5¢, 10¢, 15¢, 16¢, 17¢, 18¢

Count on. Write how much.

1.

5¢, 6¢, 7¢, 8¢, 9¢, 10¢   10¢

2.

_____¢, _____¢, _____¢, _____¢, _____¢    _____¢

3.

_____¢, _____¢, _____¢, _____¢    _____¢

4.

_____¢, _____¢, _____¢, _____¢, _____¢, _____¢    _____¢

Use with Lesson 1, text pages 353–354.

Dimes and Pennies

Name _____

Count on by 10s for dimes. | Count on by 1s for pennies.

10¢, 20¢, 30¢, 31¢, 32¢, 33¢

Count on. Write how much.

1.

10¢, 11¢, 12¢, 13¢, 14¢, 15¢

2.

_____¢, _____¢, _____¢, _____¢, _____¢, _____¢

3.

_____¢, _____¢, _____¢, _____¢, _____¢, _____¢

4.

_____¢, _____¢, _____¢, _____¢, _____¢, _____¢

Quarters and Pennies

Count on by 1s from 25¢.

25¢, 26¢, 27¢, 28¢, 29¢

Count on. Write how much.

1.

25¢, 26¢, 27¢

 27¢

2.

____¢, ____¢, ____¢, ____¢

 ____¢

3.

____¢, ____¢

 ____¢

4.

____¢, ____¢, ____¢, ____¢, ____¢, ____¢

 ____¢

Use with Lesson 3, text pages 357–358.

Count On by Dimes and Nickels

Name _____

Sort like coins and order from greatest to least value.

Then count on. 10¢, 20¢, 30¢, 35¢, 40¢

Count on. Write how much.

1.

10¢, 20¢, 30¢, 35¢, 40¢, 45¢    45¢

2.

____¢, ____¢, ____¢, ____¢, ____¢    ____¢

3.

____¢, ____¢, ____¢, ____¢, ____¢, ____¢    ____¢

4.

____¢, ____¢, ____¢, ____¢, ____¢, ____¢    ____¢

Use with Lesson 4, text pages 359–360.

Count Mixed Coins

Name _____

Sort like coins and order from greatest to least value.

Then count on.

25¢, 35¢, 45¢, 50¢, 51¢

Count on. Write how much.

1.

25¢, 35¢, 40¢, 41¢, 42¢, 43¢ — 43¢

2.

____¢, ____¢, ____¢, ____¢, ____¢, ____¢ — ____¢

3.

____¢, ____¢, ____¢, ____¢, ____¢ — ____¢

4.

____¢, ____¢, ____¢, ____¢, ____¢, ____¢ — ____¢

108 one hundred eight

Use with Lesson 5, text pages 361–362.

Equal Amounts

Name _____

| 5¢, 10¢, **15¢** | 10¢, **15¢** | 10¢, 11¢, 12¢, 13¢, 14¢, **15¢** |

Write each amount.
Circle the amounts that are equal.

1.

‸27¢‸

 ____ ¢

 ____ ¢

2.

____ ¢

 ____ ¢

 ____ ¢

3.

____ ¢

 ____ ¢

 ____ ¢

4.

____ ¢

 ____ ¢

 ____ ¢

Use with Lesson 6, text pages 365–366.

Spending Money

Name _____

Is there enough money to buy a for 47¢?

25¢, 35¢, 40¢, 41¢, 42¢, 43¢

$43¢ < 47¢$

There is not enough money to buy the . ☹

Write the amount you have. Draw ☺ or ☹
to tell if you have enough money to buy the toy.

1.

58¢

25¢, 35¢, 45¢, 55¢, 60¢

☺

2.

46¢

____¢, ____¢, ____¢, ____¢, ____¢

3.

33¢

____¢, ____¢, ____¢, ____¢, ____¢

4.

57¢

____¢, ____¢, ____¢, ____¢, ____¢

Use with Lesson 7, text pages 367–368.

One Dollar

Name _____

Skip count to show $1.

one dollar = 100 cents
$1 = 100¢

25¢, 50¢, 75¢, 100¢

Skip count. Circle to show $1.

1.

2.

3.

4.

Hour

Read the time on each clock as 3 o'clock.

Write the time shown.

1.

_____ o'clock

 1:00

2.

_____ o'clock

3.

_____ o'clock

4.

_____ o'clock

5.

_____ o'clock

6.

_____ o'clock

7.

_____ o'clock

8.

_____ o'clock

9.

_____ o'clock

10.

_____ o'clock

11.

_____ o'clock

12.

_____ o'clock

Use with Lesson 9, text pages 373–374.

Half Hour

There are 30 minutes in 1 half hour.

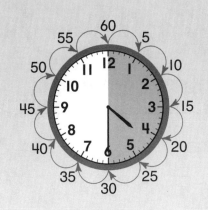

4:30

Read this time as:
4 thirty
half past 4
30 minutes after 4

Write the time in two ways.

1.

half past ____

2.

____ thirty

3.

____ minutes after ____

4.

half past ____

5.

____ thirty

6.

____ minutes after ____

7.

half past ____

Time Patterns

Name _____

This is an hour pattern.   This is a half-hour pattern.

Write or draw to complete each time pattern.
Circle to show the type of pattern.

1.

__3__ o'clock   __4__ o'clock   _____ o'clock

half hour

(hour)

2.

_____ o'clock   _____ thirty   _____ o'clock

half hour

hour

3.

_____ o'clock   _____ thirty   _____ o'clock

half hour

hour

4.

_____ thirty   _____ thirty   half past _____

half hour

hour

Use with Lesson 11, text pages 377–378.

Elapsed Time

Name _____

 9:30 to 10:30 is I hour.

Draw or write the time to show how long each activity takes.
Circle how long.

I. Read a book.

Begin at 1:30.

End at 2:30.

I half hour

(I hour)

2. Eat breakfast.

Begin at 5:30.

End at 6:30.

I half hour

I hour

3. Eat dinner.

Begin at 6:30.

End at 7:00.

6:30 to _____

I half hour

I hour

4. Do homework.

Begin at 4:00.

End at 5:00.

_____ to _____

I half hour

I hour

Estimate Time

To estimate time means to tell about how long it takes to do something.

brush your teeth

| about 1 minute |

go to the dentist

| about 1 hour |

Color to show how long.

1. make a cake

| about 1 minute |

| about 1 hour |

2. take a picture

| about 1 minute |

| about 1 hour |

3. do a puzzle

| about 1 minute |

| about 1 hour |

4. do laundry

| about 1 minute |

| about 1 hour |

5. tie a shoe

| about 1 minute |

| about 1 hour |

6. open a present

| about 1 minute |

| about 1 hour |

Use with Lesson 13, text pages 381–382.

Order Events

Many events, or activities, happen in an order.

Write morning, afternoon, or evening
to order these events.

1.

afternoon _____ _____

2.

_____ _____ _____

3.

_____ _____ _____

Ordinals to 31st

Name _____

Ten toys are on the shelf.
The ordinal of the next toy put on the shelf is 11th.

11th 12th 13th 14th 15th 16th 17th 18th 19th 20th

31st 30th 29th 28th 27th 26th 25th 24th 23rd 22nd 21st

Write the ordinal number for each toy.

1.

27th

2.

_____

3.

_____

4.

_____

5.

_____

6.

_____

7.

_____

8.

_____

9.

_____

10.

_____

11.

_____

12.

_____

Use with Lesson 15, text pages 387–388.

Calendar

Name _____

November						
Sunday	Monday	Tuesday	Wednesday	Thursday	Friday	Saturday
			1	2	3	4
5	6	7	8	9	10	11
12	13	14	15	16	17	18
19	20	21	22	23	24	25
26	27	28	29	30		

Use the calendar above to answer each question.

1. The day November 1 falls on is __Wednesday__.

2. November has _____ days.

3. The date for the first Tuesday is _____.

4. November has _____ Mondays and _____ Thursdays.

5. One week after November 15 falls on a _____.

6. The last day of November falls on a _____.

7. The day December 1 falls on is a _____.

Problem-Solving Strategy: Logical Reasoning

Name _____

Read ▸ Tom arrives at school at 8:30.
Jack arrives last.
Kate and Rachel arrive after Tom.
Who gets to school second?

Plan ▸ Make a list. Put the facts in the order that they happen.

Write ▸

When	Who
8:30	Tom
next	Kate and Rachel
last	Jack

Kate and Rachel get to school second.

Check ▸ Read the problem again to be sure your facts are in the correct order.

Use logical reasoning to solve the problem.

1. Grandpa goes to sleep at 10:00.
Amy goes to bed before Grandpa.
Justin goes to bed after Grandpa.
Who goes to bed last?

When	Who
before Grandpa	
10:00	
after Grandpa	

_____ goes to bed last.

Use with Lesson 17, text pages 393–394.

Problem-Solving Applications: Mixed Strategies

Name _____

Read ▸ **Plan** ▸ **Write** ▸ **Check**

Use a strategy you have learned.

Strategy File

Logical Reasoning
Draw a Picture
Make a Table
Choose the Operation

1. Cora's shape has 6 corners.
Paula's shape has 3 sides.
Abbey's shape has 2 more
corners than Paula's.
Circle Abbey's shape.

---

2. Tamara is thinking of a
number greater than 40.
It is an odd number.
It has more ones than tens.
What is Tamara's number?

$$37 \quad 49 \quad 51 \quad 32$$

Tamara's number is _____.

---

3. Anna is eighth in line.
Carl is 3 places behind her.
The man behind Carl is last in line.
What is Carl's position in line?

Carl is _____ in line.

---

4. Andrea has 6 🪙.
Erika has 1 🪙.
How much money do they have altogether?

They have _____ altogether.

Length and Height: Nonstandard Units

Name _____

Length is how long something is.
Height is how tall something is.

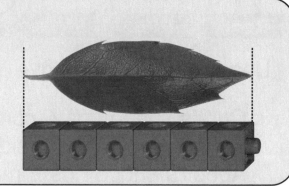

The is about 6 long.

Use to measure the length or height of each picture.

1.

about __7__

2.

about _____

3.

4.

5.

about _____   about _____   about _____

Use after Lessons 1 and 2, text pages 407–410.

Perimeter

Name _____

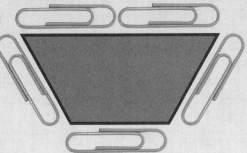

Perimeter is the distance around a figure.

There are 5 around the figure.

The perimeter is about 5 ⬚.

Use small ⬚ to find the perimeter.

1.

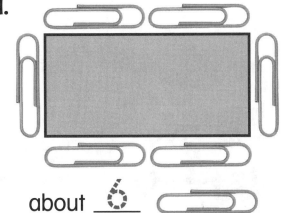

about __6__ ⬚

2.

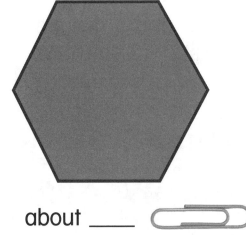

about ____ ⬚

3.

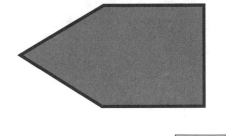

about ____ ⬚

4.

about ____ ⬚

5.

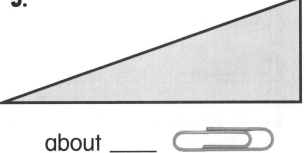

about ____ ⬚

6.

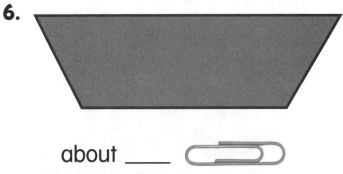

about ____ ⬚

Compare Lengths

Name _____

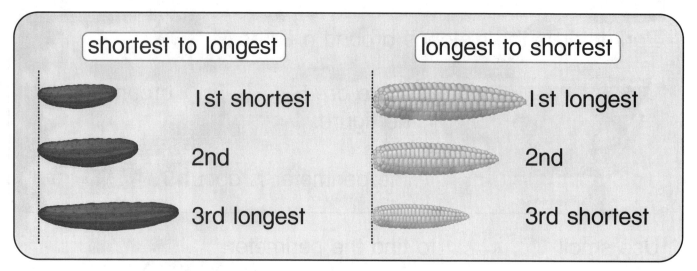

shortest to longest

1st shortest

2nd

3rd longest

longest to shortest

1st longest

2nd

3rd shortest

Compare and order the objects.
Write 1st, 2nd, and 3rd.

shortest to longest

longest to shortest

1.
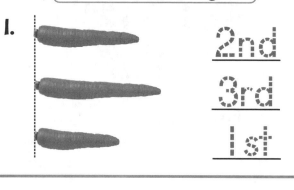

2nd

3rd

1st

4.
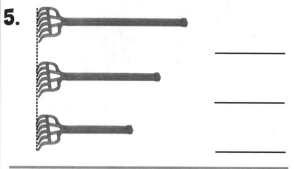

_____

_____

_____

2.

_____

_____

_____

5.
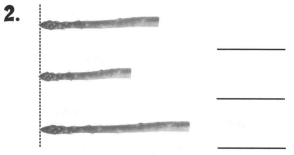

_____

_____

_____

3.
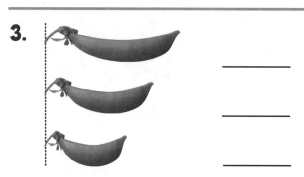

_____

_____

_____

6.
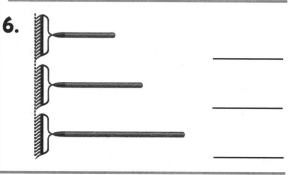

_____

_____

_____

Use with Lesson 4, text pages 413–414.

Inches

Name _____

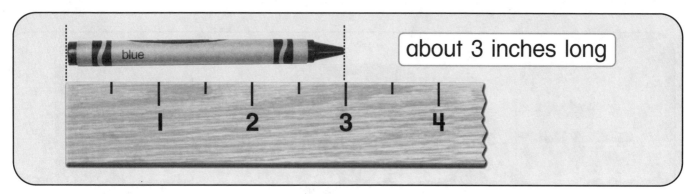

about 3 inches long

Measure the length or height of each picture in inches.

1.  about __4__ inches

2.  about ____ inches

3.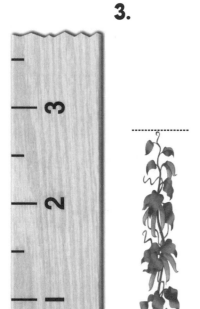

4.

5.

6.

about ____ inches

about ____ inches

about ____ inch

about ____ inches

Feet

less than 1 foot | about 1 foot | more than 1 foot

Think about these real objects.
Estimate the length of each real object.
Circle the most reasonable estimate.

1.

(more than 1 foot)

about 1 foot

less than 1 foot

2.
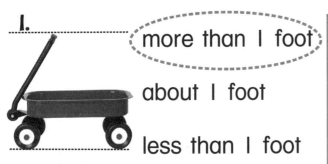

more than 1 foot

about 1 foot

less than 1 foot

3.

more than 1 foot

about 1 foot

less than 1 foot

4.

more than 1 foot

about 1 foot

less than 1 foot

5.

more than 1 foot

about 1 foot

less than 1 foot

6.

more than 1 foot

about 1 foot

less than 1 foot

Use with Lesson 9-6, text pages 417–418.

Capacity: Nonstandard Units

Name _____

Use a to estimate about how much each container holds.

about 1   about 10   about 60

Estimate about how many each real container holds.

1.

2   (10)

2.

5   50

3.

6   20

4.

4   40

5.

10   25

6.

2   10

Cups, Pints, and Quarts

2 cups = 1 pint   2 pints = 1 quart

Circle which holds more.

1.
 or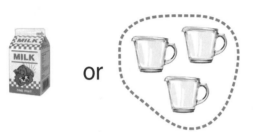

2.
 or

3.
 or

4.
 or

Write how many.

5.

2  = ____

6.

2 = ____

7.

8  = ____

8.

6 = ____

Use after Lessons 9 and 10, text pages 425–428.

Weight: Nonstandard Units

Name _____

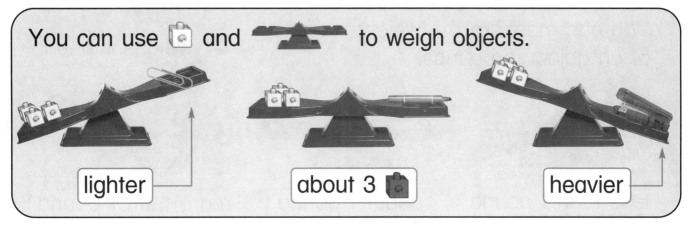

You can use 📷 and ⚖️ to weigh objects.

| lighter | about 3 📷 | heavier |

Compare the weight of these objects.
Circle the object that is heavier. ✗ the object that is lighter.

1.

2.

3.

4.

5.

6.

7.

8.

Pounds

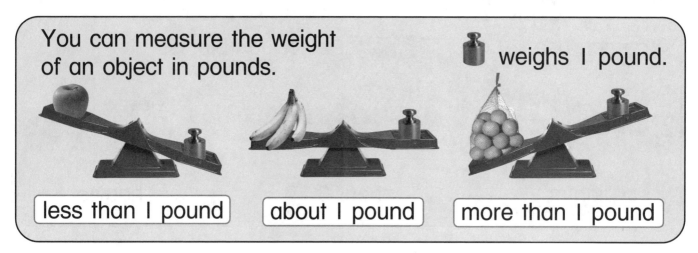

You can measure the weight of an object in pounds.

weighs 1 pound.

| less than 1 pound | about 1 pound | more than 1 pound |

Think about these real objects.
Circle about how much each object weighs.

1.
(less than 1 pound)

about 1 pound

more than 1 pound

2.
less than 1 pound

about 1 pound

more than 1 pound

3.
less than 1 pound

about 1 pound

more than 1 pound

4.
less than 1 pound

about 1 pound

more than 1 pound

5.
less than 1 pound

about 1 pound

more than 1 pound

6.
less than 1 pound

about 1 pound

more than 1 pound

Use with Lesson 12, text pages 431–432.

Centimeters

Name _____

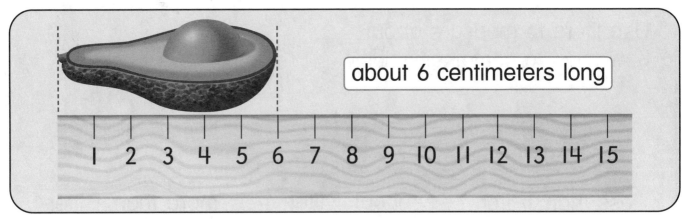

about 6 centimeters long

Use a centimeter ruler to measure the
length of each picture.

1.

about
__9__ centimeters

2.

about
____ centimeters

3.

about
____ centimeters

Measure the height in centimeters.

 **4.**

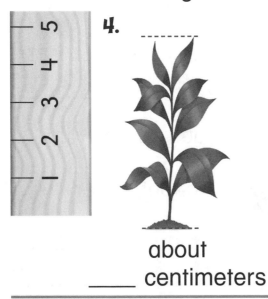

about
____ centimeters

5.

about
____ centimeters

6.

about
____ centimeters

Liters

Use liters to measure about
how much a container holds.

less than I liter

about I liter

more than I liter

Circle about how much each
real container holds.

1.

less than I liter

about I liter

(more than I liter)

2.

less than I liter

about I liter

more than I liter

3.

less than I liter

about I liter

more than I liter

4.

less than I liter

about I liter

more than I liter

5.

less than I liter

about I liter

more than I liter

6.

less than I liter

about I liter

more than I liter

Use with Lesson 14, text pages 437–438.

Kilograms

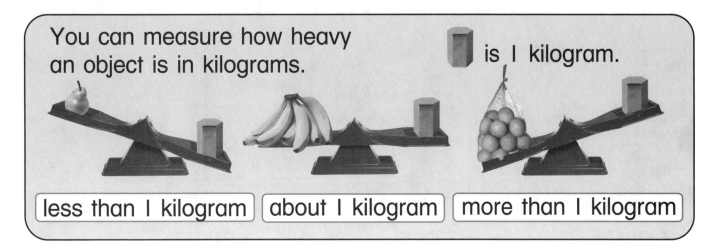

You can measure how heavy an object is in kilograms.

is I kilogram.

| less than I kilogram | about I kilogram | more than I kilogram |

Circle about how heavy.

1.

(less than I kilogram)

about I kilogram

more than I kilogram

2.

less than I kilogram

about I kilogram

more than I kilogram

3.

less than I kilogram

about I kilogram

more than I kilogram

4.

less than I kilogram

about I kilogram

more than I kilogram

5.

less than I kilogram

about I kilogram

more than I kilogram

6.

less than I kilogram

about I kilogram

more than I kilogram

Temperature; Seasons

Name _____

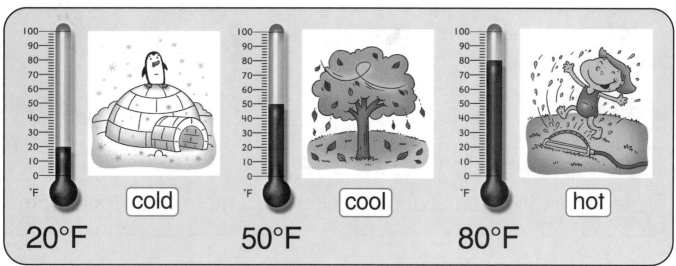

cold — 20°F

cool — 50°F

hot — 80°F

Read each thermometer. Write the temperature.

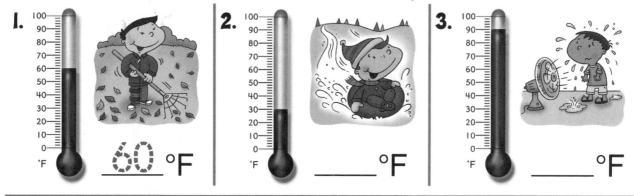

1. 60 °F

2. _____ °F

3. _____ °F

4. Draw lines to match the season with the picture.

winter

spring

summer

fall

Use after Lessons 16 and 17, text pages 441–444.

Choose a Measuring Tool

Name _____

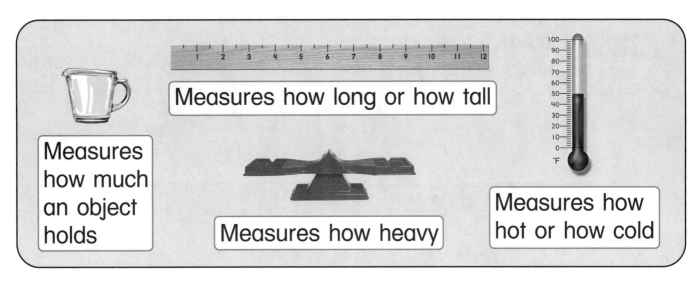

Measures how long or how tall

Measures how much an object holds

Measures how heavy

Measures how hot or how cold

Circle the tool you would use to measure.

1. How much does it hold?

2. How hot is it?

3. How much does it weigh?

4. How long is it?

5. How much does it hold?

6. How much does it weigh?

Problem-Solving Strategy:
Make a Model

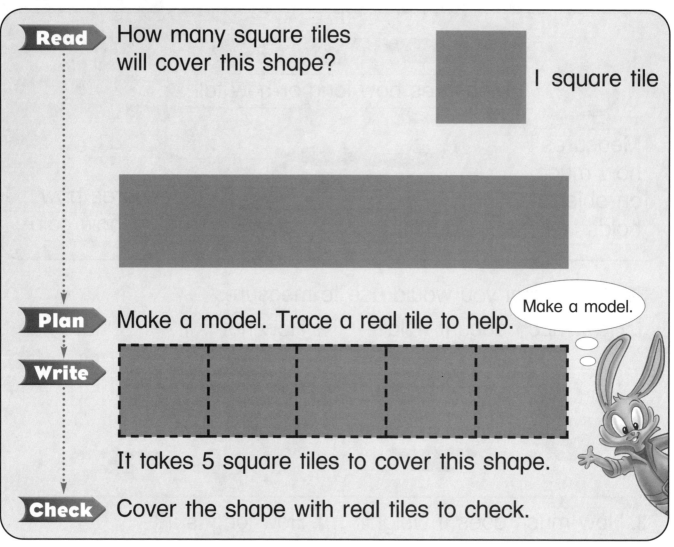

Read How many square tiles will cover this shape?

1 square tile

Plan Make a model. Trace a real tile to help.

Make a model.

Write

It takes 5 square tiles to cover this shape.

Check Cover the shape with real tiles to check.

Use ▪ to solve each question.

1. How many square tiles will cover each shape?

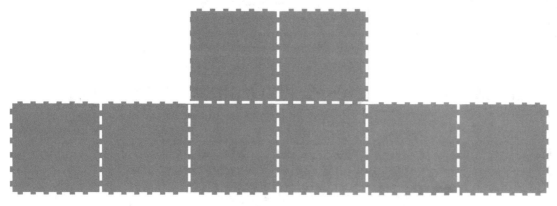

_____ ▪ will cover this shape.

Use with Lesson 19, text pages 447–448.

Problem-Solving Applications: Mixed Strategies

Name _____

Read > **Plan** > **Write** > **Check**

Use a strategy you have learned.

Strategy File

Find/Use a Pattern
Logical Reasoning
Draw a Picture
Make a Table

1. Simon saves a 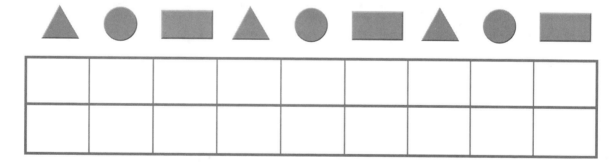 every day for 10 days. How much does he save in all?

Simon saves _____ in all.

2. Tad writes five 2-digit numbers.
They are between 44 and 66.
They all have either 5 or 0 in the ones place.
What numbers does Tad write?

_____, _____, _____, _____, _____

3. Find a pattern.
Write the same pattern using letters and numbers.

▲ ● ■ ▲ ● ■ ▲ ● ■

4. José has 7 dinner plates.
He breaks 3 plates at dinner.
How many plates does José have left?

José has ____ plates left.

Add Tens and Dimes

Name _____

1 ten	10		1 dime	10¢
+3 tens	+30		+3 dimes	+30¢
4 tens	40		4 dimes	40¢

4 tens = 40   4 dimes = 40¢

Add. Use 🪙 or ▭▭▭ to help.

1.
6 dimes
+2 dimes
8 dimes

60¢
+20¢
80¢

2.
4 tens
+3 tens
_____ tens

+ □
□

3.
5 tens
+2 tens
_____ tens

+ □
□

4.
1 dime
+4 dimes
_____ dimes

+ □
□

5.
40
+50
90

6.
20
+60

7.
80¢
+10¢

8.
10
+50

9.
20¢
+40¢

10.
70
+20

11.
30¢
+10¢

12.
60
+30

13. 30 + 40 = _____

14. 10 + 70 = _____

Use with Lesson 1, text pages 465–466.

Add Ones and Tens Using Models

Name _____

38 + 21 = ?

Model the addends. | **Add the ones.** | **Then add the tens.**

tens	ones
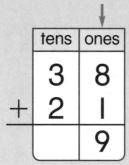	

	tens	ones
	3	8
+	2	1
		9

	tens	ones
	3	8
+	2	1
	5	9

38 + 21 = 59

Add. Use ▬▬▬ and ▪.

1.
	tens	ones
	4	2
+	2	4
	6	6

tens	ones

2.
	tens	ones
	1	2
+	3	5

tens	ones

3.
	tens	ones
	2	2
+	2	2

tens	ones

4.
	tens	ones
	4	1
+	1	5

tens	ones

5.
	tens	ones
	3	7
+	1	2

tens	ones

6.
	tens	ones
	1	4
+	4	3

tens	ones

Add Ones and Tens Without Models

Name _____

Add the ones, then add the tens.	Change the order of the addends to check the sum.

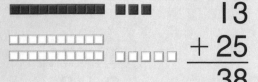

$$\begin{array}{r} 13 \\ +25 \\ \hline 38 \end{array}$$

$$\begin{array}{r} 13 \\ +25 \\ \hline 38 \end{array} \quad \begin{array}{r} 25 \\ +13 \\ \hline 38 \end{array}$$

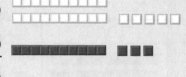

Find the sum. Change the order to check.

1.
$$\begin{array}{r} 21 \\ +56 \\ \hline 77 \end{array} \quad \begin{array}{r} 56 \\ +21 \\ \hline 77 \end{array}$$

2.
$$\begin{array}{r} 73 \\ +24 \\ \hline \end{array} \quad + \boxed{}$$

3.
$$\begin{array}{r} 50 \\ +39 \\ \hline \end{array} \quad + \boxed{}$$

4.
$$\begin{array}{r} 22 \\ +43 \\ \hline \end{array} \quad + \boxed{}$$

5.
$$\begin{array}{r} 45 \\ +12 \\ \hline \end{array} \quad + \boxed{}$$

6.
$$\begin{array}{r} 34 \\ +62 \\ \hline \end{array} \quad + \boxed{}$$

7.
$$\begin{array}{r} 23 \\ +13 \\ \hline \end{array} \quad + \boxed{}$$

8.
$$\begin{array}{r} 47 \\ +31 \\ \hline \end{array} \quad + \boxed{}$$

9.
$$\begin{array}{r} 65 \\ +24 \\ \hline \end{array} \quad + \boxed{}$$

10.
$$\begin{array}{r} 81 \\ +15 \\ \hline \end{array} \quad + \boxed{}$$

11.
$$\begin{array}{r} 43 \\ +42 \\ \hline \end{array} \quad + \boxed{}$$

12.
$$\begin{array}{r} 66 \\ +30 \\ \hline \end{array} \quad + \boxed{}$$

13.
$$\begin{array}{r} 57 \\ +40 \\ \hline \end{array} \quad + \boxed{}$$

14.
$$\begin{array}{r} 64 \\ +15 \\ \hline \end{array} \quad + \boxed{}$$

15.
$$\begin{array}{r} 28 \\ +70 \\ \hline \end{array} \quad + \boxed{}$$

Use with Lesson 3, text pages 469–470.

Add Money

11¢ + 21¢ = ?

Model each amount.

dimes	pennies

Add the pennies.

dimes	pennies
1	1
+ 2	1
	2

Add the dimes.

dimes	pennies
1	1
+ 2	1
3	2

11¢ + 21¢ = 32¢

Use 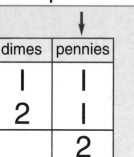 and ⬤ to add.

I.

dimes	pennies
2	1
+ 4	7
6	8

    21¢
  +47¢
   68¢

2.

dimes	pennies
3	4
+ 2	5

    34¢
  +25¢

3.   56¢
       +32¢

4.   76¢
       +13¢

5.   43¢
       +34¢

6.   42¢
       +43¢

7.   39¢
       +30¢

8.   15¢
       +44¢

9.   24¢
       +52¢

10. 82¢
       +17¢

II.   33¢
        +50¢

12.   62¢
        +12¢

Add Ones or Tens

Name _____

$52 + 2 = ?$

Start at 52.
Count on 2 ones.
$+1 \quad +1$
52, 53, 54

$52 + 2 = 54$

$52 + 20 = ?$

Start at 52.
Count on 2 tens.
$+10 \quad +10$
52, 62, 72

$52 + 20 = 72$

Add. Count on by ones or by tens.

1.
$$\begin{array}{r} 38 \\ + \ 1 \\ \hline 39 \end{array} \qquad \begin{array}{r} 38 \\ +10 \\ \hline 48 \end{array}$$

2.
$$\begin{array}{r} 11 \\ + \ 2 \\ \hline \end{array} \qquad \begin{array}{r} 11 \\ +20 \\ \hline \end{array}$$

3.
$$\begin{array}{r} 24 \\ + \ 1 \\ \hline \end{array} \qquad \begin{array}{r} 24 \\ +10 \\ \hline \end{array}$$

4.
$$\begin{array}{r} 62 \\ + \ 3 \\ \hline \end{array} \qquad \begin{array}{r} 62 \\ +30 \\ \hline \end{array}$$

5.
$$\begin{array}{r} 45 \\ + \ 4 \\ \hline \end{array} \qquad \begin{array}{r} 45 \\ +40 \\ \hline \end{array}$$

6.
$$\begin{array}{r} 57 \\ + \ 2 \\ \hline \end{array} \qquad \begin{array}{r} 57 \\ +20 \\ \hline \end{array}$$

7.
$63 + 20 =$ _____

$63 + \ 2 =$ _____

8.
$31 + \ 3 =$ _____

$31 + 30 =$ _____

9.
$37 + \ 2 =$ _____

$37 + 20 =$ _____

10.
$16 + \ 3 =$ _____

$16 + 30 =$ _____

11.
$24¢ + 30¢ =$ _____

$24¢ + \ 3¢ =$ _____

12.
$51¢ + \ 1¢ =$ _____

$51¢ + 10¢ =$ _____

Use with Lesson 5, text pages 473–474.

Nearest Ten

Is 56 closer to 50 or 60?

To find the closer number, find the nearest ten.

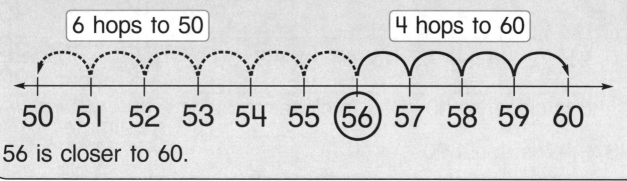

| 6 hops to 50 | | 4 hops to 60 |

50 51 52 53 54 55 (56) 57 58 59 60

56 is closer to 60.

Draw hops to find the nearest ten.

I. Is 73 closer to 70 or 80?

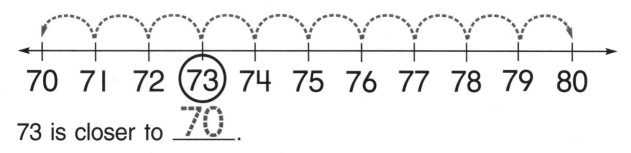

70 71 72 (73) 74 75 76 77 78 79 80

73 is closer to __70__.

2. Is 68 closer to 60 or 70?

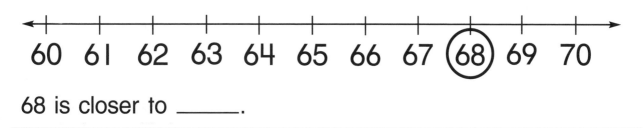

60 61 62 63 64 65 66 67 (68) 69 70

68 is closer to _____.

3. Is 24 closer to 20 or 30?

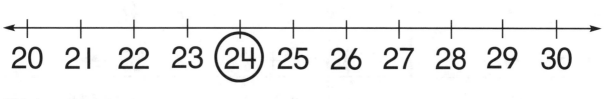

20 21 22 23 (24) 25 26 27 28 29 30

24 is closer to _____.

Estimate Sums

Estimate the sum of 43 + 49.

Find the nearest ten for each addend.

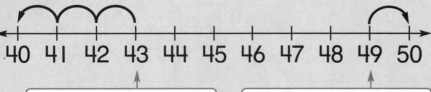

43 is closer to 40   49 is closer to 50

43 + 49 is about 90.

Then add
the nearest tens.

$$43 \longrightarrow \quad 40$$
$$+49 \longrightarrow +50$$
$$\text{about} \quad 90$$

estimate

Estimate the sum.

1. 22 → [20]
  + 41 → +[40]
  about [60]

2. 39 → [ ]
  + 32 → +[ ]
  about

3. 76 → [ ]
  + 12 → +[ ]
  about

4. 57 → [ ]
  + 17 → +[ ]
  about

5. 28 → [ ]
  + 62 → +[ ]
  about

6. 54 → [ ]
  + 23 → +[ ]
  about

7. 11 → [ ]
  + 81 → +[ ]
  about

8. 16 → [ ]
  + 71 → +[ ]
  about

9. 14 → [ ]
  + 58 → +[ ]
  about

10. 42 → [ ]
  + 53 → +[ ]
  about

11. 19 → [ ]
  + 36 → +[ ]
  about

12. 46 → [ ]
  + 37 → +[ ]
  about

Use with Lesson 7, text pages 477–478.

Regroup Ones as Tens Using Models

Name _____

Regroup 1 ten 17 ones.

Model 1 ten 17 ones.   Regroup 10 ones as 1 ten.

1 ten 17 ones = 2 tens 7 ones

Use ▬▬▬ and ▪.
Regroup 10 ones as 1 ten.

1.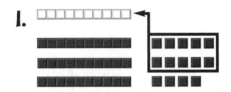

3 tens 14 ones = __4__ tens __4__ ones

2.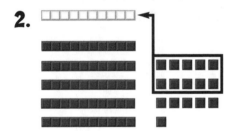

5 tens 16 ones = ____ tens ____ ones

3.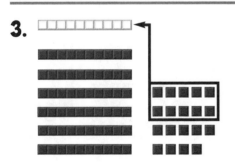

6 tens 19 ones = ____ tens ____ ones

4.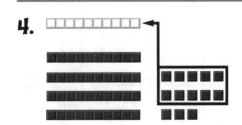

4 tens 13 ones = ____ tens ____ ones

Regroup Ones as Tens Using a Chart

Name _____

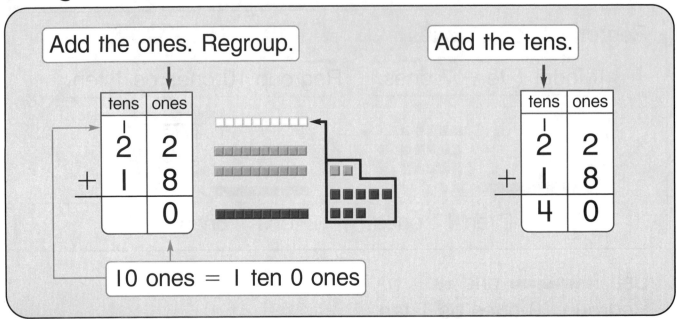

Add the ones. Regroup.

Add the tens.

tens	ones
1 2	2
+ 1	8
	0

10 ones = 1 ten 0 ones

tens	ones
1 2	2
+ 1	8
4	0

Find the sum.

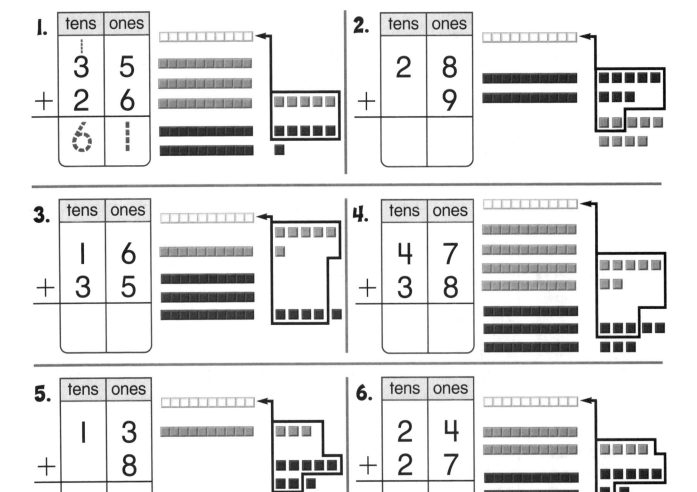

1.

tens	ones
3	5
+ 2	6
6	1

2.

tens	ones
2	8
+	9

3.

tens	ones
1	6
+ 3	5

4.

tens	ones
4	7
+ 3	8

5.

tens	ones
1	3
+	8

6.

tens	ones
2	4
+ 2	7

Use with Lesson 10, text pages 485–486.

Copyright © by William H. Sadlier, Inc. All rights reserved.

Regroup Money

Name _____

$23¢ + 19¢ = ?$

Model the amounts.
Regroup. 10 pennies = 1 dime

Add the pennies.
Regroup 10 pennies as 1 dime.
Add the dimes.

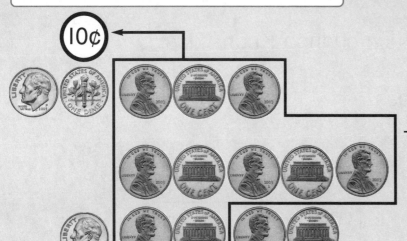

dimes	pennies
2	3
+ 1	9
4	2

$23¢$
$+19¢$
$42¢$

Use 🪙 and 🪙 to find the sum.

1.

dimes	pennies
6	3
+ 1	7
8	0

2.

dimes	pennies
3	6
+ 3	4

3.

dimes	pennies
6	4
+ 2	6

4. $26¢$
$+17¢$

5. $39¢$
$+ 8¢$

6. $51¢$
$+19¢$

7. $68¢$
$+18¢$

8. $55¢$
$+ 6¢$

9. $22¢$
$+68¢$

10. $37¢$
$+54¢$

11. $14¢$
$+79¢$

Problem-Solving Strategy:
Guess and Test

Name _____

Read ▶ Khan needs 85¢ to buy a mango. 〔45¢〕 〔65¢〕 〔55¢〕
He finds some change in his pocket.
Now he needs 30¢ to buy a mango.
How much change does Khan find in his pocket?

Plan ▶ Guess how much change Khan finds.

Write ▶ Test each guess.

45¢	65¢	55¢
+ 30¢	+ 30¢	+ 30¢
75¢	95¢	85¢

75¢ < 85¢ 95¢ > 85¢ 85¢ = 85¢
not enough   too much   ✔

Khan finds 55¢.

Check ▶ Use real coins to check.

Guess and test to find the answer. 〔1〕 〔11〕 〔21〕

1. Sarah has 5 .
Joanna has some, too.
Together they have 26 .
How many does
Joanna have?

1	11	21
+ 5	+ 5	+ 5
6	16	26

Joanna has _____ .

2. Diaz has 2 .
One costs 68¢.
How much more money
does Diaz need to buy one ?

〔48¢〕 〔18¢〕 〔58¢〕

Diaz needs _____.

Use with Lesson 12, text pages 489–490.

Problem-Solving Applications: Mixed Strategies

Name _____

 **Read** > **Plan** > **Write** > **Check**

Use a strategy you have learned.

Strategy File

Make a Table
Choose the Operation
Logical Reasoning

1. Sybil plants 10 flowers in a minute. How many flowers does she plant in 7 minutes?

Sybil plants ____ flowers in 7 minutes.

---

2. Hana has 3 dimes.
Her mom gives Hana
1 penny and 2 nickels.
How much money does Hana have then?

Hana has ____.

---

3. At the pool, 12 children use .
6 children use .
8 children use .
How many more children use than ?

____ more children use than .

---

4. The sum of two numbers is 16.
The difference between the
two numbers is 2.
What are the two numbers?

The numbers are ____ and ____.

Subtract Tens and Dimes

Name _____

To subtract 50 − 30, think 5 tens − 3 tens.

5 tens	50
−3 tens	−30
2 tens	20

2 tens = 20

To subtract 50¢ − 30¢, think 5 dimes − 3 dimes.

5 dimes	50¢
−3 dimes	−30¢
2 dimes	20¢

2 dimes = 20¢

Subtract. Use 🪙 or ▬▬▬▬ to help.

1.

9 dimes	90¢
−7 dimes	−70¢
2 dimes	20¢

2.

6 tens	
−2 tens	−
tens	

3.

4 tens	
−3 tens	−
ten	

4.

2 dimes	
−1 dime	−
dime	

5.
```
  70
 −40
  30
```

6.
```
  80¢
 −50¢
```

7.
```
  90
 −80
```

8.
```
  50¢
 −40¢
```

9.
```
  30
 −20
```

10.
```
  80¢
 −60¢
```

11.
```
  70
 −50
```

12.
```
  90¢
 −50¢
```

13. 60 − 40 = _____

14. 70¢ − 30¢ = _____

Use with Lesson 1, text pages 503–504.

Subtract Ones and Tens Using Models

Name _____

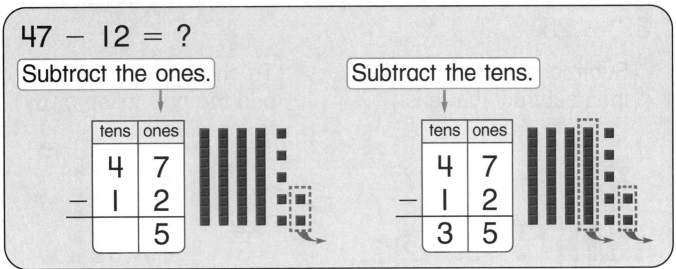

$$47 - 12 = ?$$

Subtract the ones.

tens	ones
4	7
− 1	2
	5

Subtract the tens.

tens	ones
4	7
− 1	2
3	5

Circle the ▬▬▬ and ▪ you subtract.
Write the difference.

1.
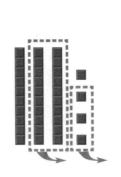

tens	ones
3	4
− 2	3

2.

tens	ones
4	8
− 2	2

3.

tens	ones
5	6
− 3	5

4.

tens	ones
2	8
− 1	3

5.

tens	ones
5	9
− 2	5

6.

tens	ones
3	5
− 1	4

Use with Lesson 2, text pages 505–506.

Subtract Ones and Tens Without Models

Name _____

$$37 - 25 = \,?$$

| Subtract the ones, then subtract the tens. | To check subtraction, add the part taken away to the difference. |

$$\begin{array}{r} 37 \\ -\,25 \\ \hline \boxed{12} \end{array}$$

$$\begin{array}{r} \boxed{12} \\ +\,25 \\ \hline 37 \end{array}$$

Subtract. Check by adding.

1.
$$\begin{array}{r} 54 \\ -\,13 \\ \hline 41 \end{array}$$
$$\begin{array}{r} \boxed{41} \\ +\boxed{13} \\ \hline 54 \end{array}$$

2.
$$\begin{array}{r} 79 \\ -\,23 \\ \hline \end{array}$$
$$+\,\boxed{}$$

3.
$$\begin{array}{r} 97 \\ -\,67 \\ \hline \end{array}$$
$$+\,\boxed{}$$

4.
$$\begin{array}{r} 67 \\ -\,13 \\ \hline \end{array}$$
$$+\,\boxed{}$$

5.
$$\begin{array}{r} 86 \\ -\,52 \\ \hline \end{array}$$
$$+\,\boxed{}$$

6.
$$\begin{array}{r} 77 \\ -\,64 \\ \hline \end{array}$$
$$+\,\boxed{}$$

7.
$$\begin{array}{r} 57 \\ -\,30 \\ \hline \end{array}$$
$$+\,\boxed{}$$

8.
$$\begin{array}{r} 32 \\ -\,11 \\ \hline \end{array}$$
$$+\,\boxed{}$$

9.
$$\begin{array}{r} 45 \\ -\,24 \\ \hline \end{array}$$
$$+\,\boxed{}$$

10.
$$\begin{array}{r} 94 \\ -\,51 \\ \hline \end{array}$$
$$+\,\boxed{}$$

11.
$$\begin{array}{r} 88 \\ -\,46 \\ \hline \end{array}$$
$$+\,\boxed{}$$

12.
$$\begin{array}{r} 55 \\ -\,20 \\ \hline \end{array}$$
$$+\,\boxed{}$$

Use with Lesson 3, text pages 507–508.

Subtract Money

Name _____

$21¢ - 11¢ = ?$

Model the subtraction.		Subtract pennies.		Subtract dimes.	

dimes	pennies
(dime) (dime)	(penny)

Subtract pennies.

dimes	pennies
2	1
− 1	1
	0

Subtract dimes.

dimes	pennies
2	1
− 1	1
1	0

$21¢ - 11¢ = 10¢$

Use (dime) and (penny) to subtract.

1.

dimes	pennies
4	5
− 2	1
2	4

$\begin{array}{r} 45¢ \\ -21¢ \\ \hline 24¢ \end{array}$

2.

dimes	pennies
3	8
− 1	6

$\begin{array}{r} 38¢ \\ -16¢ \\ \hline \end{array}$

3. $\begin{array}{r} 46¢ \\ -13¢ \\ \hline \end{array}$

4. $\begin{array}{r} 87¢ \\ -70¢ \\ \hline \end{array}$

5. $\begin{array}{r} 68¢ \\ -25¢ \\ \hline \end{array}$

6. $\begin{array}{r} 95¢ \\ -55¢ \\ \hline \end{array}$

7. $\begin{array}{r} 58¢ \\ -31¢ \\ \hline \end{array}$

8. $\begin{array}{r} 66¢ \\ -10¢ \\ \hline \end{array}$

9. $\begin{array}{r} 57¢ \\ -23¢ \\ \hline \end{array}$

10. $\begin{array}{r} 98¢ \\ -32¢ \\ \hline \end{array}$

11. $\begin{array}{r} 25¢ \\ -14¢ \\ \hline \end{array}$

12. $\begin{array}{r} 76¢ \\ -64¢ \\ \hline \end{array}$

13. $\begin{array}{r} 97¢ \\ -25¢ \\ \hline \end{array}$

14. $\begin{array}{r} 38¢ \\ -24¢ \\ \hline \end{array}$

15. $\begin{array}{r} 48¢ \\ -33¢ \\ \hline \end{array}$

16. $\begin{array}{r} 95¢ \\ -70¢ \\ \hline \end{array}$

17. $\begin{array}{r} 67¢ \\ -54¢ \\ \hline \end{array}$

Subtract Ones or Tens

$55 - 3 = ?$	$55 - 30 = ?$
Start at 55, count back by 1s.	Start at 55, count back by 10s.
$-1 \quad -1 \quad -1$	$-10 \quad -10 \quad -10$
55, 54, 53, 52	55, 45, 35, 25
$55 - 3 = 52$	$55 - 30 = 25$

Subtract mentally. Write the difference.

1.
$$\begin{array}{r} 56 \\ -4 \\ \hline 52 \end{array} \qquad \begin{array}{r} 56 \\ -40 \\ \hline 16 \end{array}$$

2.
$$\begin{array}{r} 68 \\ -3 \\ \hline \end{array} \qquad \begin{array}{r} 68 \\ -30 \\ \hline \end{array}$$

3.
$$\begin{array}{r} 49 \\ -2 \\ \hline \end{array} \qquad \begin{array}{r} 49 \\ -20 \\ \hline \end{array}$$

4.
$$\begin{array}{r} 96 \\ -30 \\ \hline \end{array} \qquad \begin{array}{r} 96 \\ -3 \\ \hline \end{array}$$

5.
$$\begin{array}{r} 88 \\ -10 \\ \hline \end{array} \qquad \begin{array}{r} 88 \\ -1 \\ \hline \end{array}$$

6.
$$\begin{array}{r} 73 \\ -2 \\ \hline \end{array} \qquad \begin{array}{r} 73 \\ -20 \\ \hline \end{array}$$

7.
$$\begin{array}{r} 60 \\ -1 \\ \hline \end{array} \qquad \begin{array}{r} 60 \\ -10 \\ \hline \end{array}$$

8.
$$\begin{array}{r} 25 \\ -20 \\ \hline \end{array} \qquad \begin{array}{r} 25 \\ -2 \\ \hline \end{array}$$

9.
$$\begin{array}{r} 65 \\ -4 \\ \hline \end{array} \qquad \begin{array}{r} 65 \\ -40 \\ \hline \end{array}$$

10.
$$\begin{array}{r} 83 \\ -30 \\ \hline \end{array} \qquad \begin{array}{r} 83 \\ -3 \\ \hline \end{array}$$

11.
$$\begin{array}{r} 44 \\ -2 \\ \hline \end{array} \qquad \begin{array}{r} 44 \\ -20 \\ \hline \end{array}$$

12.
$$\begin{array}{r} 37 \\ -1 \\ \hline \end{array} \qquad \begin{array}{r} 37 \\ -10 \\ \hline \end{array}$$

13.
$$76 - 2 = \underline{}$$
$$76 - 20 = \underline{}$$

14.
$$55 - 40 = \underline{}$$
$$55 - 4 = \underline{}$$

Use with Lesson 5, text pages 511–512.

Estimate Differences

Estimate the difference of 39 − 31.

Find the nearest ten for each.   Then subtract.

30 31 32 33 34 35 36 37 38 39 40

31 is closer to 30   39 is closer to 40

$$\begin{array}{r} 39 \rightarrow\ \ 40 \\ -\,31 \rightarrow -30 \\ \hline \text{about } 10 \end{array}$$

estimate

39 − 31 is about 10.

Estimate the difference.

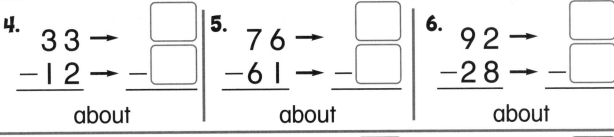

1. $\begin{array}{r} 68 \rightarrow \boxed{70} \\ -24 \rightarrow -\boxed{20} \\ \hline \end{array}$
about $\boxed{50}$

2. $\begin{array}{r} 91 \rightarrow \square \\ -19 \rightarrow -\square \\ \hline \end{array}$
about

3. $\begin{array}{r} 56 \rightarrow \square \\ -48 \rightarrow -\square \\ \hline \end{array}$
about

4. $\begin{array}{r} 33 \rightarrow \square \\ -12 \rightarrow -\square \\ \hline \end{array}$
about

5. $\begin{array}{r} 76 \rightarrow \square \\ -61 \rightarrow -\square \\ \hline \end{array}$
about

6. $\begin{array}{r} 92 \rightarrow \square \\ -28 \rightarrow -\square \\ \hline \end{array}$
about

7. $\begin{array}{r} 41 \rightarrow \square \\ -38 \rightarrow -\square \\ \hline \end{array}$
about

8. $\begin{array}{r} 87 \rightarrow \square \\ -41 \rightarrow -\square \\ \hline \end{array}$
about

9. $\begin{array}{r} 49 \rightarrow \square \\ -23 \rightarrow -\square \\ \hline \end{array}$
about

10. $\begin{array}{r} 28 \rightarrow \square \\ -21 \rightarrow -\square \\ \hline \end{array}$
about

11. $\begin{array}{r} 62 \rightarrow \square \\ -47 \rightarrow -\square \\ \hline \end{array}$
about

12. $\begin{array}{r} 83 \rightarrow \square \\ -39 \rightarrow -\square \\ \hline \end{array}$
about

Regroup Tens as Ones Using Models

Name _____

Model 2 tens 2 ones.	Regroup 1 ten as 10 ones.

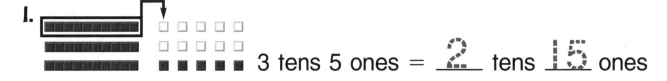

2 tens 2 ones = 1 ten 12 ones

Use ▬▬▬▬ and ■ .
Regroup 1 ten as 10 ones.

1.

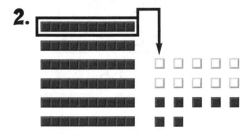 3 tens 5 ones = __2__ tens __15__ ones

2.

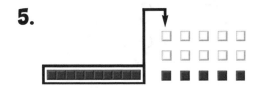 6 tens 7 ones = ____ tens ____ ones

3.

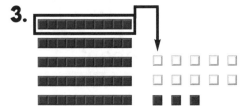 5 tens 3 ones = ____ tens ____ ones

4.

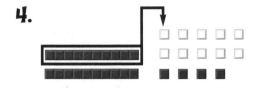 2 tens 4 ones = ____ ten ____ ones

5.

1 ten 5 ones = ____ tens ____ ones

Use with Lesson 8, text pages 519–520.

Regroup Tens as Ones Using a Chart

Name _____

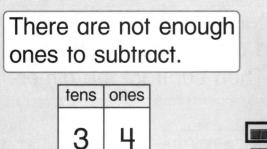

There are not enough ones to subtract.	Regroup 1 ten as 10 ones. Subtract. Begin with the ones.

tens | ones
3 | 4
− 1 | 5

3 tens 4 ones = 2 tens 14 ones

tens | ones
2
3̸ | 1̸4̸ 4
− 1 | 5
1 | 9

Regroup 1 ten as 10 ones. Find the difference.
Circle the part you take away.

1.

tens	ones
5 6̸	13 3̸
− 2	6
3	7

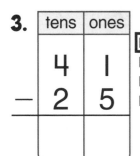

2.

tens	ones
3	5
−	8

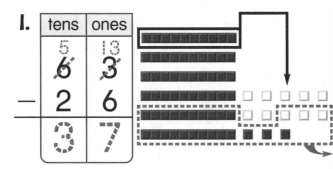

3.

tens	ones
4	1
− 2	5

4.

tens	ones
5	8
− 3	9

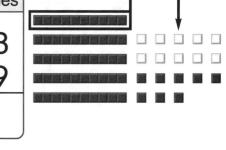

5.

tens	ones
7	6
− 2	8

6.

tens	ones
6	4
− 3	8

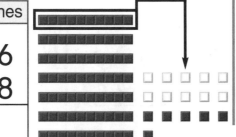

Regroup Dimes as Pennies

Name _____

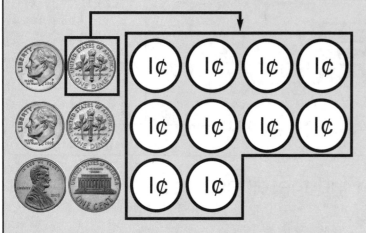

$42¢ - 24¢ = ?$

Model 42¢. Regroup 1 dime as 10 pennies.

Use the pennies from your regrouped dime to subtract the pennies. Then subtract the dimes.

dimes	pennies
3	12
~~4~~	2
− 2	4
1	8

$$\overset{3\ 12}{\cancel{4}\,2}¢ \\ -24¢ \\ \overline{18¢}$$

$42¢ - 24¢ = 18¢$

4 dimes 2 pennies = 3 dimes 12 pennies

Use 🪙 and 🪙 to find the difference.

1.

dimes	pennies
4	11
~~5~~	~~1~~
− 2	7
2	4

2.

dimes	pennies
2	6
−	8

3.

dimes	pennies
6	4
− 5	9

4.
$$28¢ \\ -\ 9¢$$

5.
$$92¢ \\ -65¢$$

6.
$$75¢ \\ -27¢$$

7.
$$33¢ \\ -29¢$$

8.
$$34¢ \\ -15¢$$

9.
$$84¢ \\ -36¢$$

10.
$$50¢ \\ -39¢$$

11.
$$51¢ \\ -48¢$$

Use with Lesson 10, text pages 523–524.

Add and Subtract Mentally

Name _____

Work from left to right.

Count back by 10s.	$53 - 30 + 3 = ?$	Count on by 1s.
Start at 53.		Start at 23.
43, 33, 23		24, 25, 26

$$23 \quad + 3 = 26$$

Add and subtract mentally.

1.
$$55 + 40 - 3 = ?$$

$$\underline{95} \bigcirc \underline{3} = \underline{92}$$

2.
$$38 - 2 + 40 = ?$$

$$\underline{\quad} \bigcirc \underline{\quad} = \underline{\quad}$$

3.
$$45 - 20 - 1 = ?$$

$$\underline{\quad} \bigcirc \underline{\quad} = \underline{\quad}$$

4.
$$17 + 30 - 3 = ?$$

$$\underline{\quad} \bigcirc \underline{\quad} = \underline{\quad}$$

5.
$$95 - 10 + 2 = ?$$

$$\underline{\quad} \bigcirc \underline{\quad} = \underline{\quad}$$

6.
$$58 + 10 - 3 = ?$$

$$\underline{\quad} \bigcirc \underline{\quad} = \underline{\quad}$$

7.
$$68 + 30 - 2 = ?$$

$$\underline{\quad} \bigcirc \underline{\quad} = \underline{\quad}$$

8.
$$22 - 20 + 1 = ?$$

$$\underline{\quad} \bigcirc \underline{\quad} = \underline{\quad}$$

Balance Number Sentences

Name _____

First solve 13 − 7.
Then find the missing number.

$$\underbracket{13 - 7} = \underbracket{? + 2}$$

$$6 = \underbracket{④ + 2}$$

$$6 = 6$$

Make each side equal.
Circle the missing number.

1. $\underbracket{7 + 5} = 9 + ?$

$$12 = 9 + ③$$

$$12 = 12$$

---

2. $? + 5 = \underbracket{2 + 12}$

$\underbracket{\underline{\quad} + 5} = \underline{\quad}$

$\underline{\quad} = \underline{\quad}$

3. $\underbracket{7 + 8} = 10 + ?$

$\underline{\quad} = \underbracket{10 + \underline{\quad}}$

$\underline{\quad} = \underline{\quad}$

---

4. $\underbracket{16 - 8} = ? + 8$

$\underline{\quad} = \underbracket{\underline{\quad} + 8}$

$\underline{\quad} = \underline{\quad}$

5. $\underbracket{8 + 5} = ? + 4$

$\underline{\quad} = \underbracket{\underline{\quad} + 4}$

$\underline{\quad} = \underline{\quad}$

---

6. $\underbracket{9 - 2} = 4 + ?$

$\underline{\quad} = \underbracket{4 + \underline{\quad}}$

$\underline{\quad} = \underline{\quad}$

7. $\underbracket{2 + 5} = ? + 3$

$\underline{\quad} = \underbracket{\underline{\quad} + 3}$

$\underline{\quad} = \underline{\quad}$

160 one hundred sixty

Use with Lesson 12, text pages 529–530.

Missing Operations

Name _____

Guess and test to find the missing signs.

9 (?) 5 (?) 4 = 8

9 (+) 5 (+) 4 = 18 ← 18 > 8

9 (−) 5 (−) 4 = 0 ← 0 < 8

9 (+) 5 (−) 4 = 10 ← 10 > 8

9 (−) 5 (+) 4 = 8 ← 8 = 8

Try + and +.
Try − and −.
Try + and −.
Try − and +.

Write the missing signs.

1. 9 (−) 5 (+) 8 = 12

2. 12 ( ) 10 ( ) 2 = 4

3. 5 ( ) 3 ( ) 9 = 17

4. 12 ( ) 5 ( ) 3 = 10

5. 8 ( ) 5 ( ) 3 = 10

6. 13 ( ) 9 ( ) 8 = 12

7. 3 ( ) 7 ( ) 2 = 12

8. 6 ( ) 6 ( ) 8 = 4

9. 11 ( ) 4 ( ) 7 = 14

10. 7 ( ) 8 ( ) 8 = 7

Problem-Solving Strategy:
Use More Than One Step

Name _____

Read Lily has 75¢.

Tammy gives Lily 13¢.

Lily spends 65¢ on .

How much money does Lily have now?

Plan Add to find how much Lily has before she buys .

Subtract the cost of from the amount Lily has.

Write

```
  7 5 ¢        8 8 ¢
+ 1 3 ¢      − 6 5 ¢
─────────    ─────────
  8 8 ¢        2 3 ¢
```

Lily has 23¢ now.

Check Use real coins to check.

---

1. Fiona counts 40  in the garden.

Rudy counts 16 more than Fiona.

Fiona picks 10 for a bouquet.

How many are left in the garden?

_____ are left in the garden.

---

2. Esther runs for 35 minutes.

Sy runs for 25 minutes.

Then Sy runs for 20 more minutes.

How much longer does

Sy run than Esther?

Sy runs _____ minutes longer than Esther.

Use with Lesson 14, text pages 533–534.

Problem-Solving Applications: Mixed Strategies

Name _____

Read ▶ **Plan** ▶ **Write** ▶ **Check**

Use a strategy you have learned.

1. Yuki counts 24 .
Paul counts 15 more than Yuki.
How many does Paul count?

Paul counts _____ .

---

2. Mr. Diego needs 29 for his students.
He has only 11 .
How many more does Mr. Diego need?

| 40 | 18 | 8 |

Mr. Diego needs _____ more .

---

3. Gary has 76¢.
He spends a quarter.
Hans has 52¢.
How much more money does Gary
need to have as much as Hans?

Gary needs _____ to have as much as Hans.

---

4. Jason has 14 goldfish. His sister
Jessica buys him some more for his
birthday. Now Jason has 27 fish.
How many fish does Jessica buy?

Jessica buys _____ fish.

Equal Parts

Name _____

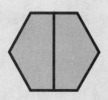 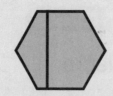

2 equal parts   2 parts not equal

Remember:
Equal parts are
the same size and
the same shape.

Circle the figure with equal parts.
Then write how many equal parts.

1.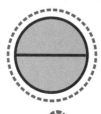

__2__ equal parts

2.

_____ equal parts

3.

_____ equal parts

4.

_____ equal parts

5.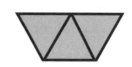

_____ equal parts

6.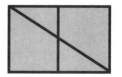

_____ equal parts

7.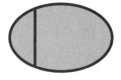

_____ equal parts

8.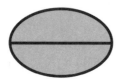

_____ equal parts

Use with Lesson 1, text pages 551–552.

One Half, $\frac{1}{2}$

| 2 equal parts of a whole are called halves | I whole | | I of 2 equal parts is $\frac{1}{2}$, or one half |

Circle the shapes that show $\frac{1}{2}$.

✗ the shapes that do not show $\frac{1}{2}$.

I.  **2.**  **3.**  **4.**

5.  **6.**  **7.** 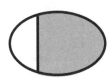 **8.**

9.  **10.** 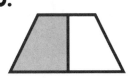 **11.** 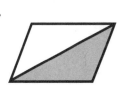 **12.**

Make halves. Color one half.

Write the fraction for the part you colored.

13.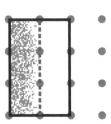

 part colored

☐ equal parts

14.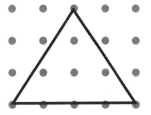

☐ part colored

☐ equal parts

15.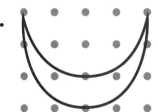

☐ part colored

☐ equal parts

One Third, $\frac{1}{3}$
One Fourth, $\frac{1}{4}$

Name _____

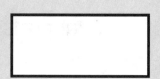 I whole

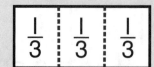 I of 3 equal parts is $\frac{1}{3}$, or one third

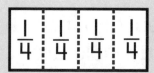 I of 4 equal parts is $\frac{1}{4}$, or one fourth

Circle the shapes that show $\frac{1}{3}$.

✗ the shapes that do not show $\frac{1}{3}$.

1.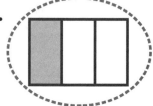

2.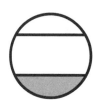

3.

4.

5.

6.

Circle the shapes that show $\frac{1}{4}$.

✗ the shapes that do not show $\frac{1}{4}$.

7.

8.

9.

10.

11.

12.

Use after Lessons 3 and 4, text pages 555–558.

Part of a Set

Name _____

What part of each set is shaded?

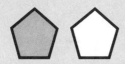

$\dfrac{1}{2}$ part shaded in all

$\dfrac{1}{2}$ is shaded.

$\dfrac{1}{3}$ part shaded in all

$\dfrac{1}{3}$ is shaded.

$\dfrac{1}{4}$ part shaded in all

$\dfrac{1}{4}$ is shaded.

What part of each set is shaded?
Write the fraction.

1. $\dfrac{1}{4}$

2.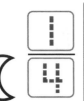

3.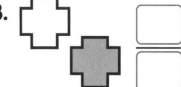

4.

5.

6.

Color one part of each set.
Write the fraction for the part you colored.

7.

8.

9.

10.

11.

12.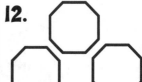

Certain, Possible, Impossible

Without looking, is it certain, possible, or impossible to pick a black marble from each bowl?

certain

possible

impossible

Is it certain, possible, or impossible to pick the marble from each bowl? Circle the correct answer.

1. pick a  | certain   possible   ⟨impossible⟩

2. pick a | certain   possible   impossible

3. pick a  | certain   possible   impossible

4. pick a  | certain   possible   impossible

5. pick a  | certain   possible   impossible

6. pick a  | certain   possible   impossible

    Use with Lesson 7, text pages 565–566.

More, Less, or Equally Likely

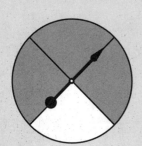 | 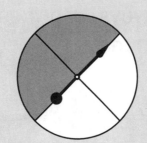 |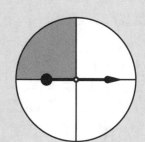

more likely to land on grey than white | equally likely to land on grey or white | less likely to land on grey than white

Which color are you more likely to land on?
Write white, grey, or black.

1.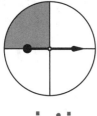

white

2.

_____

3.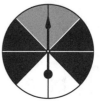

_____

Which color are you less likely to land on?

4.

black

5.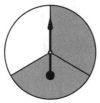

_____

6.

_____

Which color are you more likely to pick?

7.

black

8.

_____

9.

_____

Use with Lesson 8, text pages 567–568.

Arrangements

I can dress 4 different ways with these clothes.

red

yellow

blue

black

red

blue

red
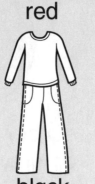
black

yellow

blue

yellow

black

Color to show the different ways you can dress.

I. purple

blue

grey

white

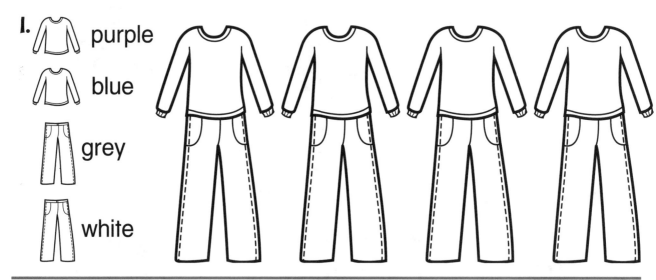

You have I yellow, I red, and I blue bead.
How many different ways can you order the
3 beads? Color to show the different ways.

2.

Use with Lesson 9, text pages 569–570.

Problem-Solving Strategy:
Make a Model/Draw a Picture

Name _____

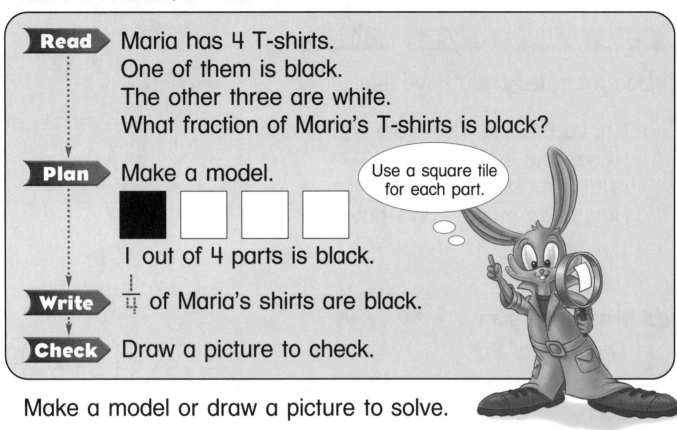

Read ▸ Maria has 4 T-shirts.
One of them is black.
The other three are white.
What fraction of Maria's T-shirts is black?

Plan ▸ Make a model.

Use a square tile for each part.

1 out of 4 parts is black.

Write ▸ $\frac{1}{4}$ of Maria's shirts are black.

Check ▸ Draw a picture to check.

Make a model or draw a picture to solve.

1. There are 5 ✏ in Adam's desk.
4 are blue.
The other is black.
What fraction of the ✏ is black?

$\frac{}{}$ of the ✏ is black.

---

2. Tim has 9 ⚾ in his bag.

8 ⚾ are new.

1 ⚾ is old.

What fraction of the ⚾ are old?

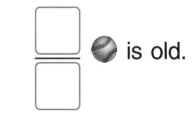 ⚾ is old.

---

3. An 🍎 is divided in 2 equal parts.
One part falls on the floor.
What fraction of the 🍎
falls on the floor?

$\frac{}{}$ of 🍎 fall on the floor.

Problem-Solving Applications: Mixed Strategies

Name _____

Read ▸ Plan ▸ Write ▸ Check

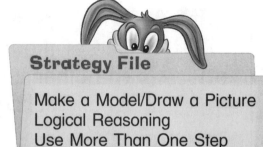

Strategy File

Make a Model/Draw a Picture
Logical Reasoning
Use More Than One Step

Use a strategy you have learned.

1. I have 5 coins. One coin is a penny.
I have the same number
of dimes as quarters.
How much money do I have?

I have _____.

---

2. Find each sum.
The sum of the
numbers inside the △ is _____.

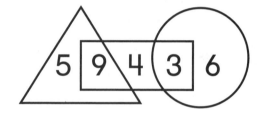

The sum of the numbers not inside the ▢ is _____.

---

3. Penny's is 7 inches long.
Andrea's is 1 foot long.
How much longer is Andrea's ?

Andrea's is _____ longer.

---

4. Adam, Trey, and Jen play 6 games of .
Adam wins 3 games. Trey wins 2 games.
Jen wins 1 game. What is the fraction
for the games Jen wins?

Jen wins ▢/▢ of the games.

Use with Lesson 11, text pages 573–574.